ECONOMIC ISSUES, PROBLEMS AND PERSPECTIVES

NON-LINEAR MODELING OF THE IMPACT OF THE CRISIS ON THE INTERACTIONS AMONG FINANCIAL MARKETS AND MACROECONOMIC VARIABLES IN CEE COUNTRIES

ECONOMIC ISSUES, PROBLEMS AND PERSPECTIVES

Additional books in this series can be found on Nova's website under the Series tab.

Additional e-books in this series can be found on Nova's website under the eBooks tab.

ECONOMIC ISSUES, PROBLEMS AND PERSPECTIVES

NON-LINEAR MODELING OF THE IMPACT OF THE CRISIS ON THE INTERACTIONS AMONG FINANCIAL MARKETS AND MACROECONOMIC VARIABLES IN CEE COUNTRIES

LUCIAN LIVIU ALBU
AND
PETRE CARAIANI
EDITORS

New York

Library of Congress Cataloging-in-Publication Data

Names: Liviu Albu, Lucian, editor. | Caraiani, Petre, editor.
Title: Non-linear modeling of the impact of the crisis on the interactions among financial markets and macroeconomic variables in CEE countries / editors, Lucian Liviu Albu and Petre Caraiani (Institute for Economic Forecasting, Romanian Academy, Romania).
Description: Hauppauge, New York: Nova Science Publishers, Inc., 2016. | Series: Economic issues, problems and perspectives | Includes index. | Description based on print version record and CIP data provided by publisher; resource not viewed.
Identifiers: LCCN 2016020727 (print) | LCCN 2016008526 (ebook) | ISBN 9781634849647 () | ISBN 9781634849326 (softcover)
Subjects: LCSH: Finance--Europe, Eastern. | Finance--Central Europe. | Finance--European Union countries. | Monetary policy--Europe, Eastern. | Monetary policy--Central Europe. | Monetary policy--European Union countries.
Classification: LCC HG186.E852 (print) | LCC HG186.E852 N66 2016 (ebook) | DDC 332.094--dc23
LC record available at https://lccn.loc.gov/2016020727

Published by Nova Science Publishers, Inc. † New York

CONTENTS

PREFACE

The last financial crisis has led to a growing interest on the mechanisms through which the stock markets and the financial markets at large influence the real economy. There has been an increasing awareness about the fact that the relationship between these two is rather nonlinear. In this context, the present book addresses the link between the financial markets and the macroeconomy within the context of the emerging markets in Central and Eastern Europe. The focus is rather on the uses of nonlinear approaches that can better uncover the dynamics during and after the crisis.

The book consists of several chapters that cover most of the topics of high interest for either academics, policy makers or the general public. The subjects range from conventional monetary policy, quantitative easing, nowcasting, to financial networks and uncertainty. There is a wide range of state of art techniques covered, including nonlinear models, event studies, financial networks, wavelets.

Overall, in the present context of the post-financial crisis, this book constitutes a step forward in the modeling of the linear and nonlinear relationships between the financial markets and the macroeconomy, especially in an unstable context and for the particular case of emerging economies in Central and Eastern Europe.

Dr. Lucian Liviu Albu, Academician
Dr. Petre Caraiani
Institute for Economic Forecasting,
Romanian Academy, Romania
December 29, 2015

ACKNOWLEDGMENT

This book contains research that was supported by a grant of the Ministry of National Education, CNCS – UEFISCDI, project number PN-II-ID-PCE-2012-4-0631, contract number 42/02.09.2013.

In: Non-Linear Modeling … ISBN: 978-1-63484-932-6
Editors: L. Liviu Albu and P. Caraiani

Chapter 1

NONLINEAR MODELLING OF THE RELATION BETWEEN FINANCIAL MARKETS AND ECONOMIC GROWTH IN THE EU

Lucian-Liviu Albu[1,*], Radu Lupu[1] and Adrian Cantemir Călin[1]

[1]Institute for Economic Forecasting,
Romanian Academy, București, Romania

ABSTRACT

Under the paradigm that in a modern economy, the financial market should be correlated with the dynamics of the macroeconomic variables, the last decade was abundant in studies that investigated the relations between these two facets of the economy. This chapter constructs an analysis that provides evidence that for more than a decade there was a strong trend of convergence for the real variables in EU but a weaker process of convergence of the stock markets. Currently we also witness discrepancies among countries and groups of countries in EU at the level of financial markets, many times irregularly correlated with the development of the real economy. The chronic underdevelopment of stock markets in CEE countries is doubled by an atypical mismatch between financial markets and macroeconomic dynamics even in the case of many western EU countries. Under these circumstances it is important

[*] E-mail: albul@ipe.ro.

firstly to find some significant parameters related to the relation between financial market and macroeconomic variables, and secondly, based on them, to re-build some possible behavioral regimes, often ignored or kept hidden in standard analysis of convergence. Our main contribution supports this paradigm by trying to highlight the manner in which few correlation regimes between market capitalisation and GDP per capita emerge, as economic growth continues to advance. Based on available high frequency data for the EU region, we also investigate the inter-country correlation both in terms of GDP growth and stock market dynamics. This approach allowed us to draw some conclusions on the phenomenon of contagion from distressed financial markets or disturbed macroeconomic environment to the rest of EU region.

Keywords: economic growth, financial markets, convergence, nonlinear model, market capitalization

INTRODUCTION

During the last period economic literature focused on the linkages between the dynamics of macroeconomic fundamentals and financial variables. Relevant contributions in this direction can be observed in Geske and Roll (1983), Chen, Roll and Ross (1986), Fama (1990), Lee (1992), Albu et al (2014), Lupu and Călin (2014), Albu et al. (2015) or Raileanu-Szeles and Albu (2015). A select portion of this academic attention has been oriented to the mechanisms that characterize the relation between the development of financial markets and economic growth. In an industrious survey, Levine (2004) argues that the development of the financial system generates positive effects that crystalize in the form of economic growth. Organizing and targeting capital from a great number of investors while in the same offering economic information, monitoring firms and measures of corporate governance, risk mitigation and upgrades in liquidity are considered by Levine (2004) as the main channels through which this growth can be achieved.

In a pioneering research Goldsmith (1969) argues that the development of the financial system had a positive contribution on economic growth. In a similar approach Greenwood and Jovanovic (1990) observe a simultaneous relation between finance and macroeconomic growth. In an investigation that relates to the previous results of Goldsmith (1969), King and Levine (1993) start from Schumpeter's idea according to which the financial system leads to economic growth and offer a cross-country empirical study. The authors incorporate indicators of financial development and report that these parameters are significantly correlated with growth, capital accumulation and the effectiveness of capital allocation.

Levine and Zervos (1998) extend the previous approach but innovate and consider the size of the stock market and liquidity as possible determinants of economic growth. They demonstrate that these elements are linked with growth and higher productivity. However, the same study argues that volatility and stock market integration are not connected with growth in a significant manner. Using quarterly data ranging from 1991 to 2004, Kenourgios and Samitas (2007) study the connection between the financial market and economic growth for the case of Poland in a cointegration approach. They report that one of the elements that generated Polish economic growth is represented by credits to the private sector.

Caporale et al. (2009) focus on ten new EU member states and try to determine the connection between financial progress and economic growth. The authors use a dynamic panel model and report that the stock and credit markets have a superficial contribution on economic growth. The results indicate a more robust influence that derives from the banking sector.

Fink et al. (2009) rely on a production function that studies the impact of credit, bond and stock markets for nine European countries and report that financial segments that have connections to the public sectors generated growth and stability during the transition period of 1996-2000.

Ayadi et al. (2013) study the linkages between the dynamics of the financial sector and economic growth focusing on the Mediterranean countries and on the 1985-2009 period. The authors report a negative correlation between credits to the private sector and bank deposits on one hand and growth on the other. In addition to this, the authors conclude that stock market size and liquidity are key elements in economic growth.

Călin (2015) also studies the possible interconnections between stock market index volatilities and macroeconomic growth for a set of ten European states, using a GARCH model and the MIDAS methodology.

REAL CONVERGENCE AND FINANCIAL MARKETS IN THE EU: EMPIRICAL EVIDENCES

One of the main goals of the European Union is convergence among its countries and regions. Indeed, during the last decades, especially after 2000 which was market by the last waves of adhering new members from Central and Eastern part of Europe, a significant convergence process in EU has been achieved. The evaluation of real convergence usually assumes the use of GDP per capita expressed in euro PPS (Purchasing Power Standard) and the grouping of countries in two categories: EU15 (old members of EU, excluding the two small island countries Cyprus and Malta) and EU11 (former Eastern communist countries which adhered to EU after 2000). For example, after 2000, a continuous convergence in EU was achieved. GDP per capita (in euro PPS), as a share of the average EU28 level, increased in EU11 from 44.4% to 65.7% in 2014 and the same variable decreased from 116.0% to 108.9% in EU15. Moreover, after 2006, the convergence in relative terms between EU11 and EU15 was accompanied by a convergence in absolute terms. Thus, the gap decreased from a maximum level of 14,594 (in 2006) to 11,807 euro per capita (in 2014). It can be observed that in all countries in EU, GDP per capita (as euro PPS) registered a positive growth between 2000 and 2014, at the EU28 level of about 39.3%.

On a country level, higher growth rates have been observed for all members of EU11 (from 45.8% in Slovenia to 192.0% in Romania) and only for three members of EU15 (51.3% in Luxembourg, 46.3% in Germany and 41.0% in Ireland). On the contrary, Italy, Greece and UK, manifested the smallest growth rates (14.2%, 18.1%, and 24.9%). At the level of EU28, GDP per capita increased in absolute terms, during the period 2000-2014, from 19,600 to 27,300 euro PPS. Higher growth was registered in eight countries of EU11 (Lithuania, Estonia, Slovakia, Latvia, Estonia, Romania, Poland and Czech Rep.) and in eight countries of EU15 (Luxembourg, Germany, Ireland, Austria, Netherlands, Sweden, Denmark and Belgium).

The convergence process in the two groups of EU states is antinomic. In the EU11 during the 2000-2014 a significant convergence process occurred expressed as a dynamics of the variation coefficient from 24.7% in 2000 to 12.5% in 2014. In the same period, inside of EU15 a divergence among countries was registered, as the variation coefficient increased from 7.0% in 2000 to 10.6% in 2014.

On the long run further convergence between the two groups of countries it is possible. According to the available published data and IMF forecast (GDP per capita expressed this time in international dollar PPP, Purchasing Power Parity), the gap between EU15 and EU11, as share of average EU28 level, already decreased from 68.4 percentage points in 2000 (115.3% against 46.9%) to 43.0 percentage points in 2014 (108.9% against 65.9%) and perhaps will continue to decrease to around 35.1 percentage points in 2020 (107.1%

against 72.0%), according to IMF forecast. Figure 1 graphically presents this dynamics.

In case of financial market, despite of a trend of convergence, there is still a larger difference among the two groups of countries in EU than in case of GDP per capita.

In terms of market capitalization as percentage of GDP the gap between EU15 and EU11 decreased from 86.7 percentage points in 2000 (102.1% in EU15 and 15.4% in EU11), to 42.2 percentage points in 2012 (64.8% in EU15 and 22.6% in EU11). In Figure 2 we observe the smallest gap between EU15 and EU11 in 2008, this being the first year of the crisis.

Given a higher volatility characteristic to financial market than to the macroeconomic time series and also given the market capitalization per capita (in euro PPS) as a share of the EU28 level, we notice a convergence between the two groups of EU. This increased in from only 7.3% in 2000 to 24.5% in 2012 and was accompanied by a decrease from 126.7% in 2000 to 119.8% in EU15.

Moreover, after 2000, the convergence in relative terms between EU11 and EU15 was generally accompanied by a convergence in absolute terms. Thus, the gap decreased from a maximum level of 21,839 in 2000 to 14,935 euro per capita, in 2012 (with a minimum level of 10,163 in 2008).

During the period 2000-2012, in all EU11 countries, except Estonia (generally being in an early stage of financial market development and ranked as "frontier markets"), a positive dynamics was observed (excepting Estonia). On the contrary, in EU15 a negative dynamics predominated (excepting Austria, Denmark, Luxembourg, Spain, and Sweden).

At the level of EU28, market capitalization per capita decreased in absolute terms, during the period 2000-2012, from 18,300 to 15,700 euro PPS. In the same period, in EU15 this indicator decreased from 23,200 to 18,800 euro PPS, but in EU11 it increased from only 1,300 to 3,800 euro PPS. A higher growth in the EU11 was registered only in Croatia (+4,900 euro PPS) and Poland (+4,600 euro PPS).

In addition to this, when it comes convergence in matter of market capitalization, as in case of GDP per capita, inside the two groups of EU there are different situations.

In EU11 in the period 2000-2012 a slow convergence was registered (in terms of the dynamics of the variation coefficient) from 60.6% in 2000 to 54.3% in 2012. In the same period, inside of EU15 there were no signs of convergence, changes in variation coefficient being insignificant (40.6% in 2000 and 40.2% in 2012).

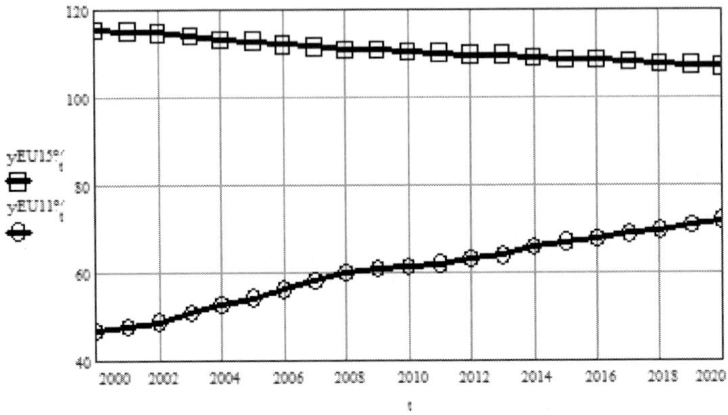

Figure 1. The gap EU15 - EU11, as share of average EU GDP per capita.

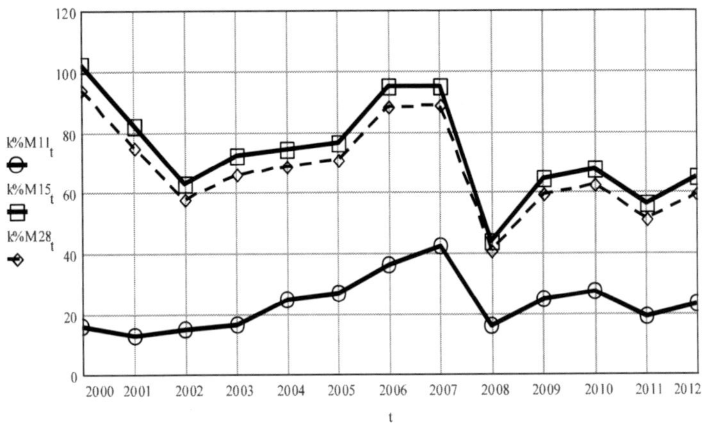

Figure 2. The gap EU15 - EU11, as market capitalization.

DISPARITIES AMONG COUNTRIES AND BEHAVIORAL REGIMES

In order to evaluate the development of a country's financial market (expressed as market capitalization per capita) related to its general level of economic development (expressed by GDP per capita), we present graphically their correlation for 2000 – 2012 in Figure 3.

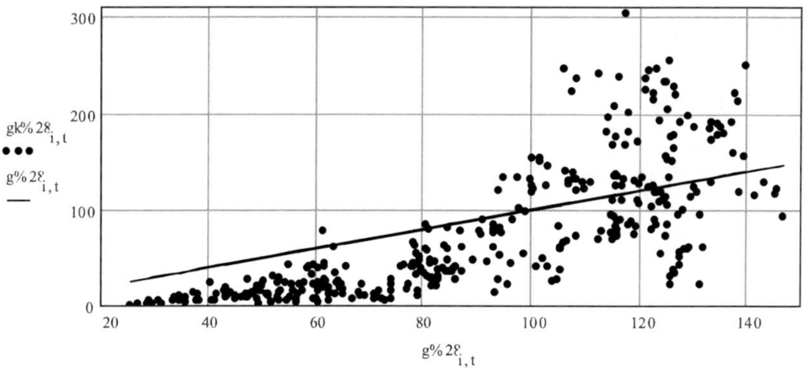

Figure 3. Correlation between the development of the financial market and the general level of economic development.

In this case, and expressing in PPS, gk%28 is the ratio between market capitalization per capita in a country and average market capitalization per capita in EU28 and g%28 is the ratio between its GDP per capita and average GDP per capita in EU28 (in Figure 3 Luxembourg was excluded).

At the level of EU28 for the period 2000-2012, the correlation between GDP per capita, y, and market capitalization per capita, k, was strongly positively (the estimated correlation coefficient is +0.807). Comparatively with their position in EU as GDP per capita, higher development of market capitalization (gk%28 > g%28) was registered for the whole analyzed period only in five western countries (as positive difference in percentage points): Luxembourg (137.0-651.3), UK (62.0-140.2), Sweden (37.2-128.0), Netherlands (15.3-109.2), and France (12.1-33.3). A similar situation was registered in Spain (for the period 2001-2012), Belgium (for the period 2006-2008 and 2012), Denmark (for 2007 and period 2009-2012), Finland (for periods 2000-2008 and 2011-2012), Croatia and Cyprus (only in 2007). In such cases it can been argued that the financial market plays a significant role in national economy.

The comparison between the situations within the two groups of countries in EU demonstrates by using individual countries data, for the entire interval (2000-2012) a strong correlation between GDP per capita and market capitalization per capita in case of EU15 (the value of estimated correlation coefficient is +0.794) but a weaker correlation in case of EU11 (the value of estimated correlation coefficient is only +0.479). Thus, as a simple rule, we may expect that an increase in the GDP per capita level to be followed by an increase in correlation coefficient between market capitalization and GDP per capita.

During the analyzed period for the EU countries we observe a stronger positive correlation between GDP per capita, y, and market capitalization per capita, k. This is the case for Poland (+0.784), Croatia (+0.693), Slovakia (+0.651), Romania (+0.639), Czech Rep. (+0.637), Spain (+0.589), Bulgaria (+0.572), Luxembourg (+0.534), Slovenia (+0.517), and Denmark (+0.516).

In the same period, a significant negative correlation has been registered in Finland (-0.466), Italy (-0.464), Netherlands (-0.242), and Estonia (-0.205).

A deeper analysis could highlight some more significant differences between the two groups of countries, as they can operate in different regimes. Thus, by putting together, on the same graphical representation, the dynamics of the values of the correlation coefficient, CORRyk, and the dynamics of the average GDP per capita (as thousand euro PPS), yM, in the period 2000-2012, it seems that there are two different regimes in which countries belonging to the two groups of EU are operating. As it is shown in Figure 4, in case of EU15, in the investigated period, there was a quasi-continuous ascending trend in the value of correlation coefficient, tending asymptotically to 1, as much as GDP per capita is increasing. Contrary, in case of EU11 group, we noticed a quasi-continuous descending trend, tending perhaps to a minimum level which is corresponding to an average GDP per capita somewhere above 17,000 euro PPS, as it is shown in Figure 5.

Figure 6 combines the two regimes on the same graphical representation. Figure 6 also incorporates as line segments the results of a nonparametric simple linear regression. The two different regimes are shown on the dashed line by the following two line segments: the first regime – the segment between points (8.694; 0.830) and (16.930; 0.277), and second regime – the segment between points (22.705; 0.808) and (28.930; 0.906).

On the dashed line there is also a third line segment which could be interpreted as a transitory regime – between points (16.930; 0.277) and (22.705; 0.808). Moreover, in order to find an alternative to discrete regimes represented by line segments, we can search for a continuous correlation function which is varying with GDP per capita, marked this time as z(y). In order to find the best candidate to approximate real registered data, we propose the following nonlinear model for the continuous function of z(y):

$$z(y) = [a / (by^2 + cy + d)] + y / (y+1)$$

where a, b, c, and d are parameters to be estimated econometrically. As output of applying a nonlinear optimization the following values for parameters were obtained:

$$\begin{bmatrix} a \\ b \\ c \\ d \end{bmatrix} = \begin{bmatrix} 667.9482925 \\ -81.18986148 \\ 2777.189194 \\ -24630.40428 \end{bmatrix}$$

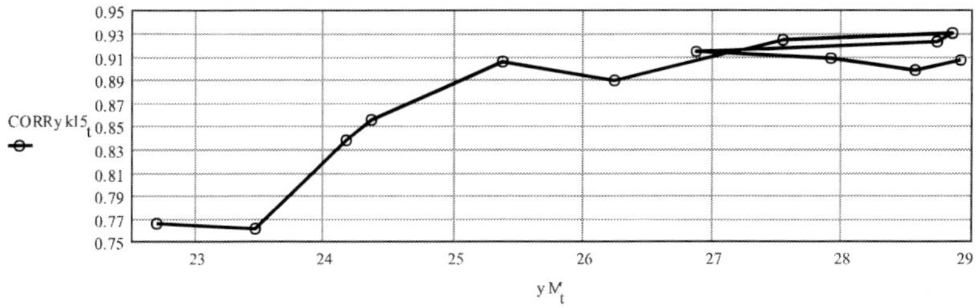

Figure 4. Dynamics of the correlation coefficient for the case of EU15.

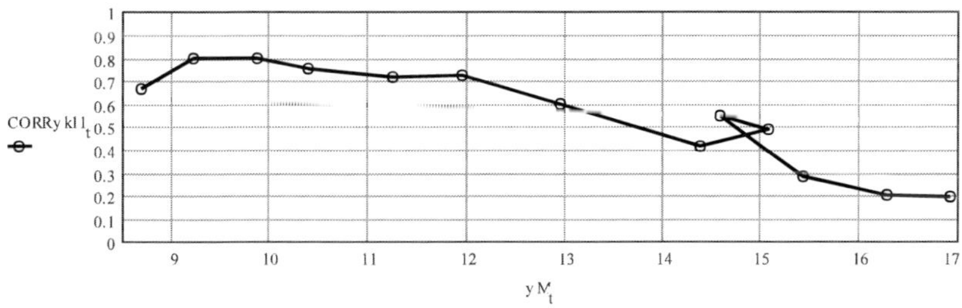

Figure 5. Dynamics of the correlation coefficient for the case of EU11.

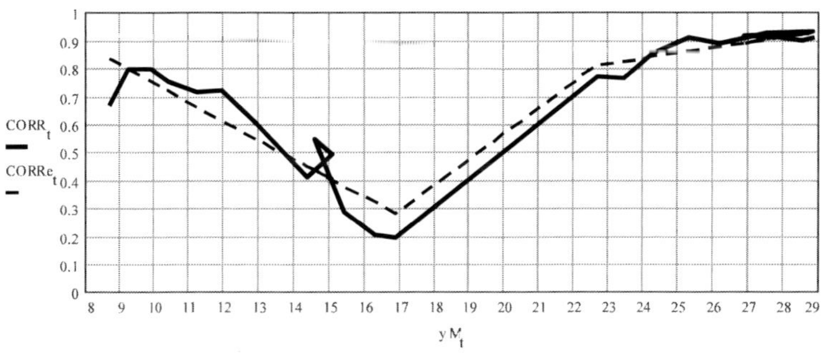

Figure 6. Three behavioural regimes in EU28.

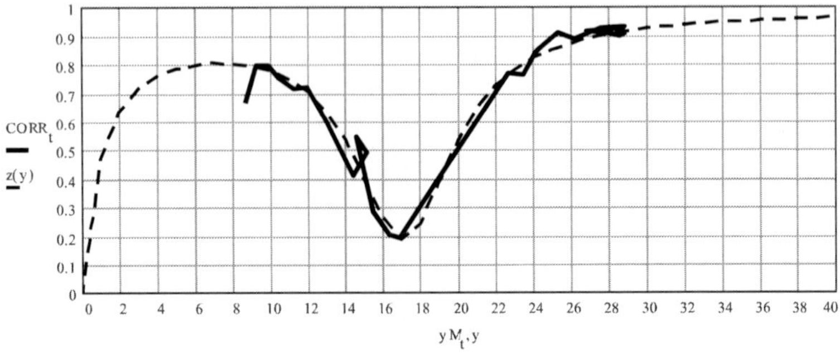

Figure 7. Representation of the nonlinear model.

In addition to this, the estimation procedure yields the following results: Coefficient of Multiple Determination (R^2) = 0.9589002877; Proportion of Variance Explained = 95.89002877%; Adjusted coefficient of multiple determination (Ra^2) = 0.9532957815; Durbin-Watson statistic = 1.579894370199.

Figure 7 shows a graphical representation of the nonlinear model (obtained by range expansion of y values on the left side to zero and on the right side to 40,000 euro per capita) is as dashed trajectory, comparatively to real registered data (solid line).

Based on the estimated nonlinear model, this time we can separate a large set of behavioral regimes. Thus, on the graph of function z(y) there are few important points eventually separating multiple regimes: two local extreme points, a maximum for y=7.35484 and a minimum for y=17.09198; two inflexion points for y=15.14797 and for y=19.0016; etc.

CORRELATIONS IN CASE OF HIGH FREQUENCY TIME SERIES

Usually, data for macroeconomic variables are published as annual time series. Only for few macroeconomic variables data are reported quarterly and/or monthly. For instance, the highest frequency in the case of GDP time series is quarterly. As an original data base we used quarterly GDP in EU countries available at Eurostat, which is referring to Gross domestic product at market prices, in million euro current prices, not seasonally adjusted.

Financial data are presented as time series with higher frequencies as for example in the case of any stock market index. In order to make a comparison with the dynamics of the GDP we selected the same quarterly data for the financial variables. Moreover, in order to ensure comparability of collected information about stock indices, we selected data for the period 2008Q3 – 2015Q1 for the most extended group of countries from the EU, namely 22 states (13 countries from EU15 and 9 countries from EU11): 1 - France, 2 - UK, 3 - Portugal, 4 - Spain, 5 - Belgium, 6 - Netherlands, 7 - Germany, 8 - Sweden, 9 - Finland, 10 - Denmark, 11 - Poland, 12 - Czech Rep., 13 - Austria, 14 - Italy, 15 - Greece, 16 - Hungary, 17 - Slovenia, 18 - Croatia, 19 - Romania, 20 - Bulgaria, 21 – Estonia, and 22 – Lithuania.

Based on data covering the period 2008Q3 – 2015Q1, for selected 22 EU countries, we estimated for each country the correlation coefficients between the dynamics of quarterly stock index, QIx, and dynamics of quarterly GDP, QY. QIx and QY were expressed as changes reported to the first term in case of the two time series (as changes against 2008Q3, noted as 100%).

At the level of the whole group of 22 countries for the investigated period there was a moderate positive correlation (+0.497).

Figure 8 shows the distribution of QIx and QY in all countries during this period (where t means quarters and i countries). On this graphical representation, a position above the solid line means that changes in QIx were higher than changes in QY.

Moreover, in Figures 9 and 10 we present the distributions by countries in each quarter of the period (27 quarters) in case of QIx and respectively in case of QY. As a general rule, we can see, for the investigated period, that a higher volatility was registered in case of QIx time series than in case of QY time series.

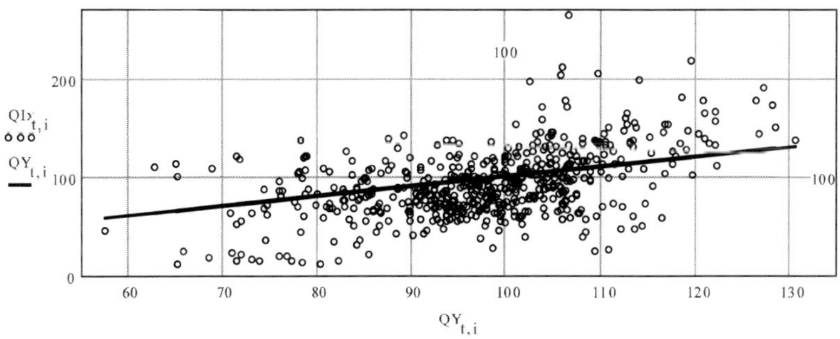

Figure 8. Distribution of QIx and QY for 22 EU countries.

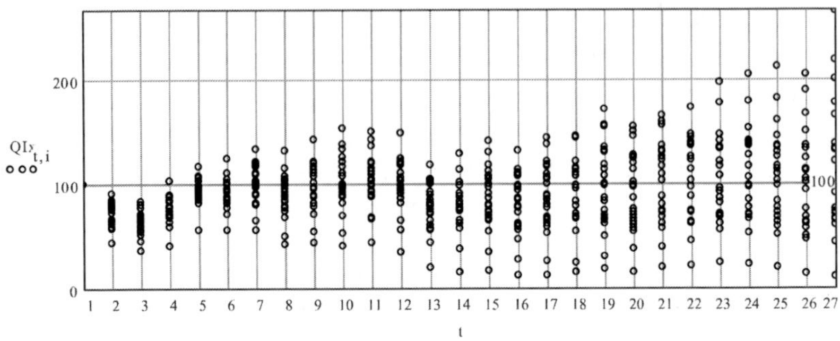

Figure 9. Distribution by country for QIx.

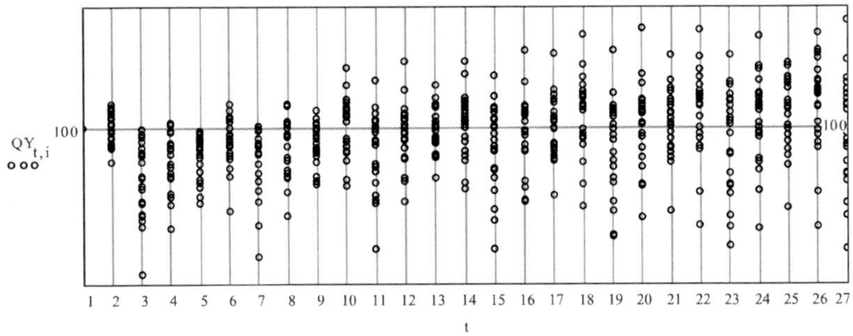

Figure 10. Distribution by country for QY.

Table 1 presents the changes between 2008Q3 and 2015Q1 (as percentage points) in QIx and in QY, and the values of the correlation coefficient for all 22 countries. Based on the data in this Table, the group of 22 countries can be separated into four subgroups, corresponding to different typologies, depending on the signs in dynamics of the two indicators, QIx and QY.

First subgroup of countries, where a positive dynamics was registered both for QIx and QY, is comprised of ten countries (eight western countries plus two eastern countries).

The second subgroup, where a negative dynamics was registered both for QIx and QY, is formed by eight countries (five CEE countries plus three Mediterranean countries).

The third subgroup, where QIx registered a positive dynamics but QY a negative dynamics, includes only three countries (two CEE countries plus one Mediterranean). Finally, fourth subgroup, where QIx registered a negative dynamics but QY a positive dynamics, is formed by only one country (Austria).

Table 1. Changes in QIx and QY and the correlation coefficient

Country	ΔQIx (%)	ΔQY (%)	corr(QIx,QY)
1 - France	32.9	9.7	0.573
2 - UK	36.7	30.7	0.793
3 - Portugal	-39.1	-5.0	0.466
4 - Spain	4.8	-3.9	0.168
5 - Belgium	98.4	14.1	0.679
6 - Netherlands	76.6	6.4	0.574
7 - Germany	64.6	12.8	0.834
8 - Sweden	116.8	19.7	0.740
9 - Finland	19.9	1.3	0.085
10 - Denmark	164.2	6.7	0.762
11 - Poland	4.4	5.1	0.574
12 - Czech Rep.	-27.0	-13.2	0.174
13 - Austria	-33.7	8.0	-0.302
14 - Italy	9.8	-1.8	-0.115
15 - Greece	-88.8	-34.8	0.828
16 - Hungary	-24.0	-15.5	-0.039
17 - Slovenia	-35.6	-10.0	0.276
18 - Croatia	-29.5	-25.3	0.233
19 - Romania	37.1	-21.7	0.292
20 - Bulgaria	-56.5	-13.6	-0.092
21 - Estonia	31.7	11.0	0.517
22 - Lithuania	36.9	-6.1	0.404

Source: Estimations based on Eurostat data.

A significant difference between financial time series and macroeconomic time series is in matter of seasonality. Generally, in first case seasonality has a small impact contrary to the latter case. Moreover, seasonality in time series of GDP has different patterns and different amplitude from country to country. Thus, in general more advanced and stable economies in EU are not so much affected by seasonality (generally less than 10 percentage points). In spite of this fact we observe an impact on GDP dynamics (generally more than 15 percentage points) for CEE countries and during the last years for Greece.

As examples of patterns, in the graphical representations of Figure 11 we observe, for the first typology, changes in quarterly time series of GDP in 1 - France, 2 - UK, and 7 - Germany, and in those of Figure 12, for the second typology, changes in quarterly time series of GDP in 15 - Greece, 19 - Romania, and 20 - Bulgaria. For the selected period, comprising of the crisis and post-crisis periods, some authors highlight the so-called phenomenon of contagion. Given this fact we should take into account information provided by data on financial market and on real economy side. Based on data covering the period 2008Q3 – 2015Q1, for selected 22 EU countries, we estimated the matrixes of correlation coefficients among countries for the dynamics of quarterly stock index, QIx, and respectively for dynamics of quarterly GDP, QY. First one is presented in Table of Annex 1, and the second one in Table of Annex 2. At the level of this group of EU, comprising 22 countries, for the whole period, there is a moderate correlation between the dynamics of stock indices and the dynamics of GDP (the value of correlation coefficient between QIx and QY is equal to +0.497). Based on data in the two matrixes, we can make some considerations regarding the contagion coming from Greece, as the most affected country by crisis. Thus, data in the 15th column could be interpreted as showing how much the situation in Greece is correlated to the situation in other countries, both on the financial market side and respectively on the real economy side. For instance, for the 2008-2015 period, changes in stock index of Greece were significantly correlated with dynamics of stock indices only for seven countries: Slovenia (+0.881), Portugal (+0.803), Czech Rep. (+0.722), Bulgaria (+0.655), Italy (+0.653), Austria (+0.598), and Spain (+0.534).

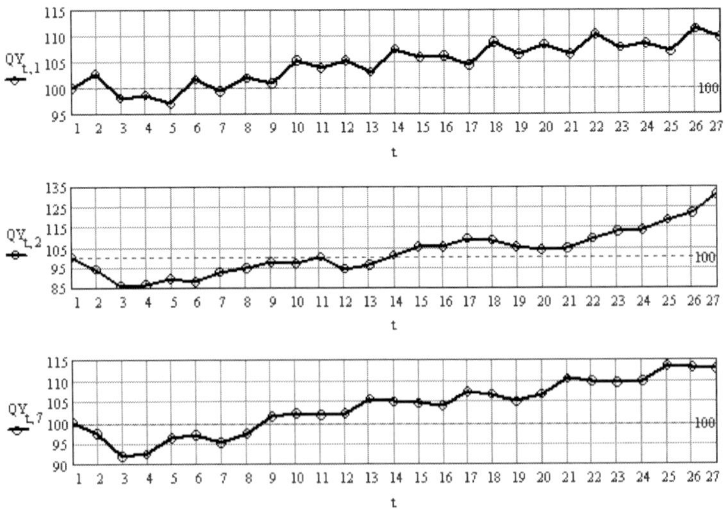

Figure 11. Patterns for developed countries.

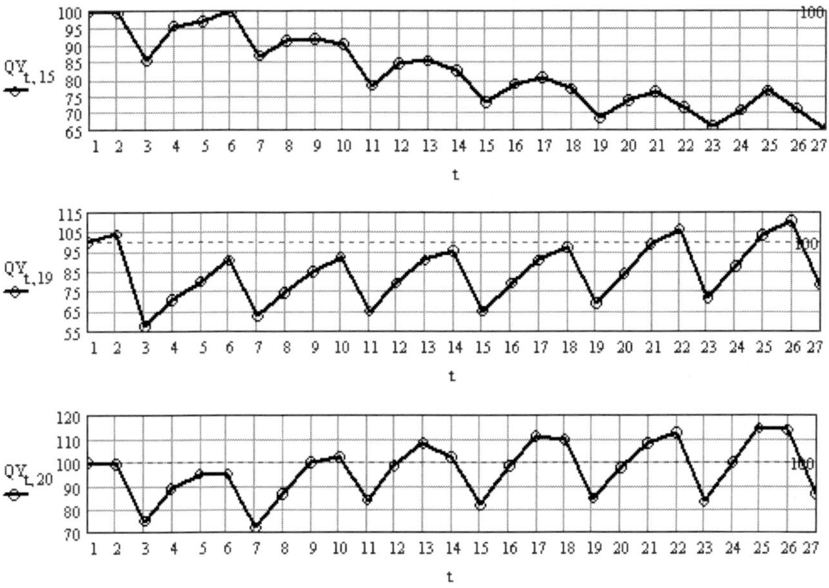

Figure 12. Patterns for CEE countries.

In an opposite way, for the following eleven countries we noticed a negative correlation with changes in the stock index of Greece: UK (-0.643), Sweden (0.638), Denmark (-0.630), Belgium (-0.571), Estonia (-0.581), Lithuania (-0.532), Germany (-0.513), Netherlands (-0.503), Romania (-0.422), Poland (-0.297), and France (-0.255). In such cases a possible interpretation is a potential protection against contagion coming from the crisis in stock market in Greece. In the same period, changes in GDP in Greece were significantly correlated with dynamics of GDP only in Portugal (+0.704), Croatia (+0.685), and Spain (+0.549), and moderately or weakly correlated with dynamics of GDP in Slovenia (+0.355), Czech Rep. (+0.237), Hungary (+0.178), Italy (+0.124), and Romania (+0.068). For most countries (13 countries) changes in GDP were negatively correlated with changes in GDP of Greece: France (-0.803), UK (-0.793), Germany (-0.782), etc. Again, for this last group of countries it was perhaps a sort of reaction against contagion coming from the Greek economy.

ANNEX 1. MATRIX OF CORRELATION COEFFICIENTS FOR QIX

CORR_QIx=

	1	2	3	4	5	6	7	8	9	10	11	12	13	14	15	16	17	18	19	20	21	22
1	1.000	0.840	-0.167	0.560	0.883	0.947	0.946	0.882	0.834	0.868	0.677	-0.125	0.292	0.503	-0.255	0.104	0.082	-0.030	0.932	0.294	0.568	0.802
2	0.840	1.000	-0.409	0.130	0.876	0.899	0.903	0.932	0.475	0.874	0.743	-0.414	0.034	0.036	-0.643	0.031	-0.375	-0.011	0.904	-0.079	0.809	0.927
3	-0.167	-0.409	1.000	0.498	-0.570	-0.432	-0.435	-0.466	0.096	-0.578	0.099	0.730	0.786	0.607	0.803	0.705	0.705	0.620	-0.311	0.631	-0.239	-0.249
4	0.560	0.130	0.498	1.000	0.223	0.354	0.302	0.229	0.793	0.203	0.294	0.524	0.566	0.936	0.534	0.336	0.756	0.191	0.385	0.711	-0.188	0.148
5	0.883	0.876	-0.570	0.223	1.000	0.973	0.962	0.940	0.610	0.977	0.511	-0.436	-0.109	0.119	-0.571	-0.198	-0.239	-0.269	0.886	-0.064	0.610	0.804
6	0.947	0.899	-0.432	0.354	0.973	1.000	0.981	0.966	0.714	0.966	0.613	-0.336	0.024	0.251	-0.503	-0.070	-0.154	-0.157	0.931	0.057	0.626	0.845
7	0.946	0.903	-0.435	0.302	0.962	0.981	1.000	0.949	0.691	0.960	0.618	-0.350	0.058	0.233	-0.513	-0.099	-0.183	-0.180	0.927	0.054	0.648	0.826
8	0.882	0.932	-0.466	0.229	0.940	0.966	0.949	1.000	0.600	0.961	0.670	-0.396	-0.031	0.108	-0.638	-0.047	-0.301	-0.121	0.895	-0.084	0.692	0.875
9	0.834	0.475	0.096	0.793	0.610	0.714	0.691	0.600	1.000	0.600	0.453	0.182	0.436	0.768	0.155	0.145	0.485	0.031	0.722	0.574	0.203	0.483
10	0.868	0.874	-0.578	0.203	0.977	0.966	0.960	0.961	0.600	1.000	0.545	-0.422	-0.137	0.106	-0.630	-0.220	-0.285	-0.268	0.882	-0.084	0.596	0.798
11	0.677	0.743	0.099	0.294	0.511	0.613	0.618	0.670	0.453	0.545	1.000	0.156	0.509	0.309	-0.297	0.557	-0.068	0.536	0.719	0.277	0.715	0.822
12	-0.125	-0.414	0.730	0.524	-0.436	-0.336	-0.350	-0.396	0.182	-0.422	0.156	1.000	0.660	0.665	0.722	0.657	0.716	0.674	-0.202	0.671	-0.412	-0.256
13	0.292	0.034	0.786	0.566	-0.109	0.024	0.058	-0.031	0.436	-0.137	0.509	0.660	1.000	0.717	0.598	0.763	0.658	0.702	0.154	0.765	0.180	0.205
14	0.503	0.036	0.607	0.936	0.119	0.251	0.233	0.108	0.768	0.106	0.309	0.665	0.717	1.000	0.653	0.446	0.828	0.294	0.323	0.821	-0.171	0.113
15	-0.255	-0.643	0.803	0.534	-0.571	-0.503	-0.513	-0.638	0.155	-0.630	-0.297	0.722	0.598	0.653	1.000	0.381	0.881	0.302	-0.422	0.665	-0.581	-0.532
16	0.104	0.031	0.705	0.336	-0.198	-0.070	-0.099	-0.047	0.145	-0.220	0.557	0.657	0.763	0.446	0.381	1.000	0.391	0.856	0.057	0.438	0.241	0.252
17	0.082	-0.375	0.705	0.756	-0.239	-0.154	-0.183	-0.301	0.485	-0.285	-0.068	0.716	0.658	0.828	0.881	0.391	1.000	0.299	-0.079	0.811	-0.444	-0.271
18	-0.030	-0.011	0.620	0.191	-0.269	-0.157	-0.180	-0.121	0.031	-0.268	0.536	0.674	0.702	0.294	0.302	0.856	0.299	1.000	-0.009	0.476	0.231	0.210
19	0.932	0.904	-0.311	0.385	0.886	0.931	0.927	0.895	0.722	0.882	0.719	-0.202	0.154	0.323	-0.422	0.057	-0.079	-0.009	1.000	0.205	0.645	0.845
20	0.294	-0.079	0.631	0.711	-0.064	0.057	0.054	-0.084	0.574	-0.084	0.277	0.671	0.765	0.821	0.665	0.438	0.811	0.476	0.205	1.000	-0.138	0.048
21	0.568	0.809	-0.239	-0.188	0.610	0.626	0.648	0.692	0.203	0.596	0.715	-0.412	0.180	-0.171	-0.581	0.241	-0.444	0.231	0.645	-0.138	1.000	0.871
22	0.802	0.927	-0.249	0.148	0.804	0.845	0.826	0.875	0.483	0.798	0.822	-0.256	0.205	0.113	-0.532	0.252	-0.271	0.210	0.845	0.048	0.871	1.000

ANNEX 2. MATRIX OF CORRELATION COEFFICIENTS FOR QY

CORR_QY =

	1	2	3	4	5	6	7	8	9	10	11	12	13	14	15	16	17	18	19	20	21	22
1	1.000	0.828	-0.261	-0.016	0.968	0.901	0.885	0.931	0.876	0.930	0.868	0.274	0.871	0.463	-0.803	0.368	0.047	-0.417	0.430	0.447	0.887	0.704
2	0.828	1.000	-0.342	-0.285	0.727	0.663	0.915	0.755	0.653	0.839	0.731	0.104	0.760	0.103	-0.793	0.248	0.048	-0.323	0.342	0.350	0.840	0.708
3	-0.261	-0.342	1.000	0.758	-0.121	-0.050	-0.246	-0.283	0.060	-0.040	0.098	0.557	-0.028	0.582	0.704	0.598	0.654	0.621	0.512	0.383	-0.227	-0.064
4	-0.016	-0.285	0.758	1.000	0.147	0.329	-0.270	-0.139	0.279	0.103	0.205	0.527	0.030	0.785	0.549	0.591	0.525	0.329	0.491	0.316	-0.075	-0.014
5	0.968	0.727	-0.121	0.147	1.000	0.919	0.811	0.899	0.905	0.917	0.882	0.353	0.882	0.601	-0.692	0.457	0.141	-0.348	0.506	0.531	0.847	0.668
6	0.901	0.663	-0.050	0.329	0.919	1.000	0.662	0.744	0.838	0.838	0.831	0.295	0.730	0.645	-0.584	0.446	0.096	-0.412	0.478	0.389	0.743	0.556
7	0.885	0.915	-0.246	-0.270	0.811	0.662	1.000	0.872	0.793	0.906	0.825	0.293	0.912	0.259	-0.782	0.392	0.181	-0.184	0.494	0.563	0.921	0.823
8	0.931	0.755	-0.288	-0.139	0.899	0.744	0.872	1.000	0.844	0.898	0.824	0.372	0.848	0.385	-0.778	0.349	0.094	-0.284	0.369	0.492	0.853	0.717
9	0.876	0.653	0.060	0.279	0.905	0.838	0.793	0.844	1.000	0.935	0.904	0.618	0.915	0.712	-0.487	0.687	0.454	0.010	0.736	0.747	0.900	0.851
10	0.930	0.839	-0.040	0.103	0.917	0.838	0.906	0.893	0.935	1.000	0.926	0.499	0.930	0.551	-0.629	0.586	0.345	-0.106	0.640	0.656	0.926	0.832
11	0.868	0.731	0.098	0.205	0.882	0.831	0.825	0.824	0.904	0.926	1.000	0.597	0.914	0.680	-0.494	0.733	0.312	-0.041	0.744	0.705	0.834	0.752
12	0.274	0.104	0.557	0.527	0.353	0.295	0.293	0.372	0.618	0.499	0.597	1.000	0.520	0.762	0.237	0.856	0.728	0.640	0.774	0.796	0.360	0.505
13	0.871	0.760	-0.028	0.030	0.882	0.730	0.912	0.848	0.915	0.930	0.914	0.520	1.000	0.563	-0.587	0.634	0.351	-0.002	0.729	0.799	0.921	0.853
14	0.463	0.103	0.582	0.785	0.601	0.645	0.259	0.385	0.712	0.551	0.680	0.762	0.563	1.000	0.124	0.800	0.496	0.229	0.760	0.672	0.373	0.372
15	-0.803	-0.793	0.704	0.549	-0.692	-0.584	-0.782	-0.778	-0.487	-0.629	-0.494	0.237	-0.587	0.124	1.000	0.178	0.355	0.685	0.068	-0.036	-0.700	-0.474
16	0.368	0.248	0.598	0.591	0.457	0.446	0.392	0.349	0.687	0.586	0.733	0.856	0.634	0.800	0.178	1.000	0.738	0.567	0.940	0.850	0.504	0.624
17	0.047	0.048	0.654	0.525	0.141	0.096	0.181	0.094	0.454	0.345	0.312	0.728	0.351	0.496	0.355	0.738	1.000	0.766	0.705	0.719	0.324	0.544
18	-0.417	-0.323	0.621	0.329	-0.348	-0.412	-0.184	-0.284	0.010	-0.106	-0.041	0.640	-0.002	0.229	0.685	0.567	0.766	1.000	0.533	0.554	-0.088	0.225
19	0.430	0.342	0.512	0.491	0.506	0.478	0.494	0.369	0.736	0.640	0.744	0.774	0.729	0.760	0.068	0.940	0.705	0.533	1.000	0.908	0.609	0.721
20	0.447	0.350	0.383	0.316	0.531	0.389	0.563	0.492	0.747	0.656	0.705	0.796	0.799	0.672	-0.036	0.850	0.719	0.554	0.908	1.000	0.651	0.767
21	0.887	0.840	-0.227	-0.075	0.847	0.743	0.921	0.853	0.900	0.926	0.834	0.360	0.921	0.373	-0.700	0.504	0.324	-0.088	0.609	0.651	1.000	0.937
22	0.704	0.708	-0.064	-0.014	0.668	0.556	0.823	0.717	0.851	0.832	0.752	0.505	0.853	0.372	-0.474	0.624	0.544	0.225	0.721	0.767	0.937	1.000

Conclusion

The economic and political convergence is considered as one of the main objectives for the achievement of prosperity within the European Union. Measured at the macroeconomic level, the concept of contagion became a directed economic phenomenon, usually as a gauge for economic integration. Weather, as a consequence of its economic importance, the phenomenon of contagion became an important element in the assessment of efficiency of political measures, its features for the dynamics of financial markets have been analyzed only independently, as part of financial integration achieved by the free movement of capital and direct access to listed securities. This chapter establishes the settlement for the development of a study of the implications of the macroeconomic convergence inside the European Union on the dynamics of financial markets in this region. After a description of the dynamics of convergence for the group of EU countries we highlight the fact that the market capitalization revealed similar levels of contagion as in the case of macroeconomic dynamics, i.e. a low level of contagion for the EU11 countries and no contagion for the EU15. An important finding was the fact that the correlation between the GDP per capita and market capitalization per capita are strongly positively correlated at the EU 28 level, which shows that the financial market integration is achieved through economic contagion. The dynamics of the correlations between the two above mentioned measures were found to be highly directly dependent on the dynamics of average GDP per capita, showing that the financial markets tend to better reflect the macroeconomic realities when the economic situation is better for the case of the EU15.

However, for EU11 these connections are reversed. Using a nonlinear model we succeeded to identify the existence of multiple regimes and two inflexion points. A study of the distribution of the financial variables at each point in time for which we obtained macroeconomic data (available due to the high frequency feature of this data) revealed a set of four typologies concerning the connections between the stock market dynamics and the quarterly GDP.

Lastly, we show the importance of seasonality in the dynamics of these time series as well as the levels of correlations that reveal the phenomenon of contagion spreading from the Greek economy.

ACKNOWLEDGMENT

This study was supported by a grant of the Ministry of National Education, CNCS – UEFISCDI, project number PN-II-ID-PCE-2012-4-0631.

REFERENCES

Albu, Lucian Liviu, Radu Lupu, and Adrian Cantemir Călin, 2015. "Interactions between financial markets and macroeconomic variables in EU: A nonlinear modeling approach", ERSA conference papers ersa15p685, European Regional Science Association.

Albu, Lucian Liviu, Radu Lupu, and Adrian Cantemir Călin, 2014. "A Nonlinear Model to Estimate the Long Term Correlation between Market Capitalization and GDP per capita in Eastern EU Countries", *Journal of Economic Computation and Economic Cybernetics Studies and Research,* 3: 5-22.

Ayadi, Rym, Emrah Arbak, Sami Ben-Naceur, and Willem Pieter De Groen, 2013. "Financial Development, Bank Efficiency and Economic Growth across the Mediterranean*", MEDPRO Technical Report No. 30/March,* 2013.

Caporale, Guglielmo Maria, Christophe Rault, Robert Sova, and Anamaria Sova, 2009. "Financial Development and Economic Growth: Evidence from Ten New EU Members", Economics and Finance Working Paper Series, Working Paper No. 09-37.

Călin, Adrian Cantemir, 2015. "Connection of European Economic Growth with the Dynamics of Volatility of Stock Market Returns", *Financial Studies,* 19(1): 53 - 66.

Chen, Nai-Fu, Richard Roll, and Stephen A. Ross, 1986. "Economic forces and the stock market", *Journal of Business,* 59: 383-403.

Fama, Eugene F., 1990. "Stock Returns, Expected Returns and Real Activity", *Journal of Finance,* 45: 1089-1108.

Fink, Gerhard, Peter Haiss, and Goran Vukšić, 2009. "Contribution of financial market segments at different stages of development: Transition, cohesion and mature economies compared", *Journal of Financial Stability,* 5(4): 431–455.

Geske, Robert, and Richard Roll, 1983. "The Fiscal and Monetary Linkage between Stock Returns and Inflation", *Journal of Finance,* 38(1): 7-33.

Goldsmith, Raymond William, 1969. Financial Structure and Development. New Haven: Yale University Press.

Greenwood, Jeremy, and Boyan Jovanovic, 1990. "Financial Development, Growth, and the Distribution of Income", *Journal of Political Economy,* 98(5): 1076-1107.

Kenourgios, Dimitris, and Aristeidis Samitas, 2007. "Financial Development and Economic Growth in a Transition Economy: Evidence for Poland", *Journal of Financial Decision Making,* 3(1): 35-48.

King, Robert G., and Ross Levine, 1993. "Finance and Growth: Schumpeter Might Be Right", *Quarterly Journal of Economics,* 108: 717-738.

Lee, Bong-Soo, 1992. "Casual Relations among Stock Returns, Interest Rates, Real Activity, and Inflation", *Journal of Finance,* 47(4): 1591-1603.

Levine, Ross, 2004. "Finance and Growth: Theory and Evidence", *NATIONAL BUREAU OF ECONOMIC RESEARCH*, Working Paper 10766.

Levine, Ross, and Sara Zervos, 1998. "Stock Markets, Banks, and Economic Growth", *American Economic Review,* 88(3): 537-558.

Lupu, Radu, and Adrian Cantemir Călin, 2014. "A mixed frequency analysis of connections between macroeconomic variables and stock markets in Central and Eastern Europe", *Financial Studies,* 18(2): 69-79.

Raileanu-Szeles, Monica, and Lucian Albu, 2015. "Nonlinearities and divergences in the process of European financial integration", *Economic Modelling,* 46(C): 416-425.

In: Non-Linear Modeling … ISBN: 978-1-63484-932-6
Editors: L. Liviu Albu and P. Caraiani

Chapter 2

THE EASTERN AND CENTRAL EUROPEAN FINANCIAL MARKET REACTION TO UNCONVENTIONAL MONETARY POLICY

Lucian-Liviu Albu, Radu Lupu and Adrian Cantemir Călin*
Institute for Economic Forecasting,
Romanian Academy, Bucharest, Romania

ABSTRACT

Despite their apparent general acceptance among decision makers, the implementation of the new strategies in monetary policy rendered analysts' opinions seemingly split between fundamental rejection arguments and clear urgency for action. An important stream of research aims at investigating the shape of the general consensus attained by the market participants and tries to quantify it with various econometric techniques. The analysis in this chapter relies on the foundation that, due to their efficiency in reflecting news and perceptions, the dynamics of liquid financial instruments uncovers relevant information about the consensus investigated at the moment of monetary policy decisions announcements. In order to measure the market reaction, we perform a volatility and direction of change analysis by using an event study to observe the reaction of the benchmark stock indices, bonds and CDS

* Corresponding author: Adrian Cantemir Călin. E-mail: cantemircalin@ipe.ro.

contracts of the Eastern and Central European markets, as response to both quantitative easing decisions in the most developed economies and the tapering decisions in the US. In pursuit of a proper characterization of the financial markets in this region, we compare these reactions to those of the correspondent financial instruments from the developed countries and draw conclusions about the degree of market integration and contagion generated thereof that characterizes this region.

Keywords: event-study, quantitative easing, tapering, volatility impact

INTRODUCTION

Albu et al. (2014) among others observe that central banks conduct monetary policy through the use of short term nominal interest rates. This conventional approach succeeds in influencing real short term rates and through this channel, a wide range of economic variables. In addition to this, by guiding the interest rate towards a certain point, central banks adjust inflation according to their objectives, determine liquidity and also influence asset prices.

This type of perspective is efficient in terms of inducing monetary impetus in normal economic conditions and also in times of economic deterioration. However, severe economic disturbances push interest rates to a near zero level. Given the normal cycles of monetary mass circulation, these nominal rates can't be reduced below zero and this limits the power of conventional methods and thus the intervention competence of central banks.

In the context of the financial meltdown of 2007-2009 that led interest rates near zero, central banks were forced to pursue alternative monetary policies in order to stimulate economic recovery. These alternative solutions, often referred to as quantitative easing, assume the expansion of the balance sheet of the bank in order to fight the problems of the financial sector, decrease interest rates and finally establish a sound flow of credit options for companies and individuals.

UNCONVENTIONAL MONETARY POLICY

Quantitative easing wasn't an innovation specific to the aftermath of the recent financial crisis. From a historic perspective, it originates from the endeavors carried out by the *Bank of Japan (BOJ)* during the 2001-2006 period. During this time frame, the prices expressed as CPI manifested a drop that in conjunction with an economic recession (negative growth rates, bankruptcy of financial institutions, unstable financial system) and with the outcome of the IT bubble stimulated the BOJ to develop a new monetary policy framework. The bank had already lowered the rate to zero in 1999, adopting the so-called ZIRP (zero interest rate policy).

In March 2001, BOJ was the first central bank that tried monetary measures entitled quantitative easing (QEP) in order to prevent further reductions of prices and restore economic growth.

Ugai (2007) comments on the fact that the BOJ approach had three main objectives:

- To modify the target for money market operations to the CABs (current account balances) retained by affiliated BOJ institutions;
- To continue the liquidity provisions until the core CPI showed an yearly increase
- To expand the acquisitions of long-term JBSs (Japanese government bonds)

The first BOJ initiative during March 2001 was the expansion of the CAB target to a value higher than the required reserve level. As the economic conditions worsened, the target was continually expanded, peaking at 36 trillion ¥ in 2004. The CAB target was accomplished by an extensive purchase program that targeted JGBs. This action grew from the initial level of 400 billion ¥ per month to 1200 billion ¥ by the autumn of 2002.

The period between July 2003 and 2006 was marked by acquisitions of targeted asset-backed securities in order to highlight the efficiency of the monetary policy. As the CPI begun to manifest a stable growth, the BOJ decided to exit quantitative easing, keeping the rate at zero percent (Ugai (2007)).

Building on this experience, the BOJ announced in December 2008 the decision to conduct a new round of quantitative easing (QEP2). The first measure consisted in an unlimited lending policy for commercial banks. This represented the birth of the SFOS (special-funds-supplying operations). In the same period the bank decided to engage new acquisitions of Japanese government bonds (Călin (2015, a).

Fawley and Neely, (2013) offer a solid survey of the history of the QEP 2 marking the most relevant landmarks of the program. In the last quarter of

2010 the Asset Purchase Program was launched, aiming at the reduction of the overnight call rate to a value between 0 and 0.1%. This initiative had as objective the reduction of long term rates and risk premium.

The next measure came in the fall of 2012 and consisted in the SBLF (Stimulating Bank Lending Facility) which by the end of the program implied a total of 15 trillion ¥. At the end of 2014, BOJ decided to further expand its QE by accelerating the rate of growing the monetary base to 80 trillion ¥ per year and continuing the acquisitions of financial instruments at a greater pace.

This orientation toward unconventional policies generated a powerful wave of academic interest that focused on the effects of quantitative easing on the financial system. Key contributions in this direction have been developed by Bernanke et al. (2004), Ugai (2007), and Shiratsuka (2010).

Kimura and Small (2004) test the rebalancing effects that derived from the BOJ QEP policy. They observe significant and positive influences that lowered risk premiums on government and superior government bonds.

In another investigation focusing on the QEP, Oda and Ueda (2005) study the influence of the ZIRP and of the monetary easing on Japanese long term interest rates. Building on the model of Oda and Kobayashi (2003), the authors find that the QEP was successful in determining reductions of the interest rates.

More recently, Bowman et al. (2015) examine the influence of the QEP on the development of bank lending. Using data from 2000 to 2009, the authors observe a positive and relevant effect of the liquidity injections on the level of lending.

Using quarterly data from 1981, Kimura and Nakajima (2013) analyze both moments of BOJ quantitative easing (2001-2006 and the programs conducted from 2010). They use a TPT-VAR approach that incorporates inflation, bank reserves, output gap, long term interest rate and short term interest rate and assume that the coefficients and relation in the TPT-VAR follow an AR (1) process. In this modeling setup, the authors observe monetary policy shocks and report that QE determined reductions in long-term interest rates.

Hayashi and Koeda (2014) use a regime-switching structural vector autoregression procedure that treats monetary policy endogenously. They incorporate three variables, namely monthly inflation rate, output gap and policy rate. The authors conclude that the expansion of reserves amplifies inflation and output.

Other VAR approaches can be found in Shibamoto and Tachibana (2014) and Tachibana (2015). Both studies follow the effects of BOJ QE on macroeconomic variables and they both report significant effects.

Lupu and Călin (2014 a) rely on an event study methodology for the examination of the effects of Japanese QE announcements on CEE sovereign CDSs. Using data for the 2005-2013 interval, the authors demonstrate the presence of abnormal returns generated by the above mentioned announcements.

The Bank of England also responded to the intensification of the financial crises of 2008. In a similar way to the other major central financial institutions, the BA adopted a mixture of conventional and unconventional measures. The main quantitative easing tool in this case was the program of asset acquisitions.

The first quantitative easing initiative was the launch of the *Asset Purchase Facility Fund-APF* at the beginning of 2009, which had as main objectives the stimulation of demand by lowering the cost of financing and price stabilization. The first purchases had a 50 billion £ limit and were oriented to private assets, corporate bonds and short term gilts. BOE also purchased commercial paper at a spread superior to the OIS rates. In addition to this, the bank announced in the same year that the APF program was extended to the sum of 75 billion £, value that in a few months rose to 200 billion £. All these actions were focused on the expansion of money supply and on the formation of a demand that would be in concordance with the inflation objective.

BOE decided to continue the quantitative easing in the fall of 2011. Under suspicions of not meeting the inflation objective, the bank grew the purchase level with another 75 billion £. The following year, the level was again raised to 325 billion £. Given a hesitant evolution of the GDP, the bank decided on another supplementation of the QE programs, this time with 50 billion £ (Fawley and Neely, (2013)).

In an early contribution, Meier (2009) surveys the BOE quantitative easing choices offering a theoretical explanation of its potential reverberations on the UK economy. A similar contribution is brought by Dale (2010) who reviews the first year of QE activity focusing on transmission channels and on the effects observed at that point.

Joyce, Tong and Woods (2011) conduct a well-documented analysis of BOE's quantitative easing following the impact on government bonds and other types of assets. They report a clear impact on assets prices arguing that gilt yields were reduced by approximately 100 basis points. These results are confirmed in a parallel study developed by Joyce et al. (2011). Focusing again on the influence on assets prices, the authors use an event study framework and notice again the 100 basis points reduction which they relate to portfolio balancing effects.

The impact of British QE on assets prices is also observed in Bridges and Thomas (2012). They use a model based on money demand and supply and find that the impact of the initial injection of 200 billion £ was compensated by other monetary shocks. Despite this fact, the authors report that QE led to an increase in money supply of 8%. From this point Bridges and Thomas (2012) use a monetarist approach discussing the determinants of money supply and demand and use this perspective to estimate a reduction of yields of about 150 basis points for 2010. The same intervention period is observed by Lyonnet and Werner (2012). This study does not focus on assets prices, but offers an investigation on the effects of QE on nominal GDP. The authors do not succeed in finding evidence that the British monetary policy conducted in 2009 had a direct influence on national economic growth.

Kapetanios et al. (2012) examine also the macroeconomic impact of the first wave of British QE, trying to observe the influence of low interest rates on the economy in general. Starting from the results of Joyce et al. (2011), they use a battery of VAR models and discover that the QE had a maximum growth effect on the GDP of 1.5% and a growth effect on inflation of 1.25%.

Albu et al. (2014 a) investigate the impact of a large set of QE announcements belonging to the Bank of England, ECB, FED and BOJ on nine CEE sovereign CDSs. Using ARMA-GARCH based event study setup they observe that the BOE QE announcements have an important influence of CDS dynamics.

Joyce and Spaltro (2014) chose a different perspective than the above mentioned studies and target the impact of BOE's QE on the bank lending process and in general on bank balance sheets. The study expands the model put foreword by Kashyap and Stein (1994) and generates a partial equilibrium two period framework capable of capturing the properties of the lending channel. Relying on a panel of non-public data, Joyce and Spaltro (2014) demonstrate that the QE has generated developments in bank lending activities.

Lupu and Călin (2014 b) focus on an analysis on the simultaneity of regime change in the evolution of 14 currency pairs that contain the British pound. The authors use a battery of 48 QE announcements made public by the bank in the 2011-2014 period and a two state Markov Switching model. The study shows an important degree of simultaneity in the regime shifts which allows the conclusion that these changes are the result of the quantitative easing promoted by the BOE.

Steely (2015) studies the dynamics of British government bonds returns around the episodes of quantitative easing in order to determine possible influences on the markets. The results show that QE reduces the cost of trading and stabilizes return evolution. In addition to this, Steely (2015) argues that investors could have obtained excessive returns in the vicinity of QE events.

The first reaction from the *European Central Bank (ECB)* came in August 2007 when it decided to inject 95 billion euro in order to ensure the necessary capital required by commercial banks. The first quantitative easing initiative came however in October 2008 in the form of unlimited capital flows for commercial banks at a fixed rate. This unlimited lending operation depended on commercial bank collateral. This action became known as fixed rate tender full allotments (FRFA). In order to complement these changes, the ECB reduced the interest rate from 4.25% to 1% until May 2009.

In addition to the FRFA measures, the bank got involved in asset acquisitions. These were oriented to the purchase of covered bonds and other elements of sovereign debt from the euro area. These covered bond purchase programs (CBPPs) were supplemented further in May 2009 when the bank decided to purchase an additional package of bonds totaling 60 billion euro (Fawley and Neely (2013)).

Another important landmark in the ECB's involvement in quantitative easing came in 2010 and consisted in the launch of the SMP (Securities Markets Program) which was dedicated to acquisitions of bonds from the secondary market. The purpose of this initiative was to boost liquidity on those markets that exhibited deficiencies and to develop the transmission channels of the monetary policy (Fawley and Neely, (2013)).

In 2011 the ECB extended the CBPP and LTROs in order to increase liquidity, but market participants speculated that this was a maneuver to finance the acquisition of sovereign debt.

The SMP was converted into the Outright Monetary Transaction (OMT) program in 2012. Fawley and Neely, (2013) argue the fact that these transactions were oriented towards the acquisition of European sovereign debt from the secondary markets and that in a similar way to the SMPs they did not influence the monetary base.

In the second part of 2014, president Mario Draghi announced that the bank was about to purchase a wide range of assets in order to encourage growth.

At present the European QE program is called the Extended Asset Purchase Program (EAPP) and it is built on three main axes: the *Asset Backed Securities Purchase Program, the Covered Bond Purchase Program* - CBPP3 and the *Public Sector Purchase Program – PSPP*. Călin (2015 a) notes that the total value of the EAPP reaches 60 billion euro per month and that the PSPP is its largest contributor having dedicated 50 billion euro.

Peersman (2011) investigates the macroeconomic influences of the unconventional monetary policy focusing on the euro area. By using a VAR model capable of detecting disturbances, Peersman (2011) argues that QE initiatives have a permanent effect on asset prices.

Albu et al. (2014 b) build on their previous approach put foreword in Albu et al. (2014 a) by isolating it to the case of the ECB quantitative easing. Using a more complex set of QE announcements, an event study framework and a series of sovereign European CDSs, they find solid and significant influences deriving from the previously mentioned announcements.

Szczerbowicz (2014) evaluates the impact of the unconventional measures taken by the ECB on borrowing costs, both for governments and banks. The author uses a series of event-based regressions to measure and compare the effects of asset acquisitions. The results indicate that the SMP, OMT, CBPP 1 and 2 and the LTROs, generated important reductions of government borrowing costs.

De Grawe and Yuemeni (2015) discuss the possibility of a riskless European QE policy. They consider that this can be done if for the bonds purchased by the ECB the interest paid by states is refunded. This move can also protect against the default risk of any of the member states.

In a study with a similar topic, Cherubini and Violi (2015) consider a battery of financial tools and political initiatives for ECB's quantitative easing, offering a securization framework. With the use of a Gaussian copula approach, the authors present a procedure for computing the probability distribution of potential credit losses.

Sosvilla-Riveroa and Fernández-Fernández (2015) investigate the influence of the QE practices of the ECB and Federal Reserve on the dollar-euro exchange rate. The results indicate the fact that ECBs QE announcements and implementation generated an appreciation of the dollar.

Quantitative easing begun in the US in the autumn of 2008 with the establishment of the Commercial Paper Funding Facility (CPFF). This was a strategy that offered short term liquidity boosts with a total dimension of 738 billion dollars.

Three main phases characterize the development of the *Federal Reserve* Quantitative Easing: QE1, QE2 and QE2.

QE1 started in November 2008 when Fed announced that it was aiming to purchase debt of government-sponsored enterprises of about 100 billion dollars. These initiative was supplemented by the acquisition of mortgage-backed securities worth 500 billion dollars.

An additional series of purchases followed in March 2009 and consisted in 100 billion dedicated to GSE debt, 750 billion to MBSs and 300 billion long term Treasuries (Fullwiler and Wray (2010)).

After a brief hiatus, QE was back into force in 2010 with the new program entitled QE2. In November that year, the bank decided to orient 600 billion dollars towards the purchase of Treasuries. The main objective of the program was to reduce long term interest rates and to keep inflation within the projected intervals.

In the fall of 2011 QE 2 got an upgrade under a constant panic of a new wave of recession. This new purchase phase was also aiming at long term treasuries. The program was called Maturity Extension Program and Reinvestment Policy and it is better known as Operation Twist.

Operation Twist got its own extension in 2012 that assumed further acquisitions of long term treasuries totaling 267 billion dollars. Given a slow response from the labor market, Federal Reserve initiated the QE 3 program in September 2012. This marked a change in perspective for the bank who established monthly acquisition levels. Therefore, the Fed decided to buy 40 billion dollars of MBS and 45 billion dollars of treasuries for an indefinite time span.

This QE status-quo held until May 2013 when Ben Bernanke first mentioned the possibility of reducing the acquisition program. The news generated an important wave of uncertainty which translated into a rise in interest rates and great volatility on assets markets. Bernanke's speech hinting on a premature exit from QE generated the term of "tapering" which describes the gradual reduction of the Fed's unconventional initiatives.

On 18 December 2013 the bank announced the first QE reduction with the sum of 10 billion dollars monthly, arriving at the 75 billion level. On 29 January 2014 a further reduction was announced, which marked the beginning of a continuously descending trajectory that came to an end on 29 October 2014 (Călin 2015 a).

As Călin (2015 a) observes in his extensive survey, a large part of the literature that studies Federal Reserve's quantitative easing considers the effects of the first large scale asset purchase programs. In general, these studies aim to discover the impact of QE on interest rates. Thus, relevant results derive from the works of: Doh (2010), Gagnon et al. (2011) or D'Amico et al. (2012).

In an early research Doh (2010) considers the efficiency of the treasuries large scale asset purchases through a preferred-habitat model and demonstrates that these measures can reduce returns on the long run.

D'Amico and King focus on Fed's 2009 programs and find that the purchase operations caused an average drop of 3.5 basis points in the day they were announced. Furthermore, the program as a whole tends to lower the return curve with about 50 basis points.

Gagnon et al. (2011) consider the implementation of the LSAPs showing the channels through which they can support the economy. In an event-study approach the authors find that the Fed policy managed to decrease the 10 year term premiums with a value raging between 30 and 100 basis points. Besides this fact, Gagnon et al. (2011) report that LSAPs had an even greater impact on long term interest rates, MBSs and agency debt.

Krishnamurthy and Vissing-Jorgensen (2011) focus on both QE1 and QE2 in order to determine their influence on interest rates. Using as well an event study methodology build on daily frequencies, the authors find an important contraction of the nominal interest rates for high grade long term securities. These results are confirmed by D'Amico et al. (2012) who find that the 300 billion dollars LSAP of 2009 resulted in a 35 basis point return reduction.

Li and Wei (2013) follow the same topic and develop a term structure model with no arbitrage for the assessment of term premium effects of Fed's LSAPS. They show that QE1, QE2 and the maturity extension program led to a cumulate reduction of 100 basis points for the 10 year Treasury yields.

Gertler and Karadi (2013) study all QE1, QE2 and QE3 LSAPs with the help of a macroeconomic model. The results hint to the fact that risky purchases are more efficient than bond purchases and that the outcome of the LSAPs depend on the stability of the zero lower bound.

Tapering has also become a topic in the literature that convers unconventional monetary policies. Eichengreen and Gupta (2013) bring forth an early investigation of the tapering measures used by the Fed and observe that tapering talk had a profound negative effect on the markets of those emerging states that appreciated their currency during the QE period. The reaction of emerging states is also observed in Aizenman et al. (2014) which conclude that the stronger emerging countries were influenced more by the tapering communications. The topic is extended in Dahlhaus and Vasishtha

(2014), research that focuses on the tapering effect on portfolio transmission to emerging states.

Călin (2015 b) analyzes the reaction of currency markets to official communications coming from the major four central banks. The results demonstrate the fact that the considered currency pairs are seriously affected in terms of volatility by the official statements covering quantitative easing and tapering. From another perspective Călin (2015 c) tries to determine the effects of tapering talk on the US real estate market and obtains moderate traces of influence.

Table 1. The instruments for the developed markets

Equity Indices		Sovereign Bonds		Sovereign CDS	
1	AEX all share	1	Austria bonds	1	Germany CDS
2	ATX - Austrian traded index	2	Belgium bonds		France CDS
3	BEL 20	3	Canada bonds	3	Greece CDS
4	DAX 30 performance	4	Denmark bonds	4	Ireland CDS
5	Euro STOXX	5	Eurobond bonds	5	Belgium CDS
6	France CAC 40	6	Finland bonds	6	Denmark CDS
7	FTSE 100	7	France bonds	7	Norway CDS
8	FTSE latibex all share	8	Germany bonds	8	Spain CDS
9	FTSE MIB index	9	Greece bonds	9	Sweden CDS
10	IBEX 35	10	Ireland bonds	10	Netherlands CDS
11	Ireland SE overall	11	Italy bonds	11	Austria CDS
12	Luxembourg SE general	12	Malta bonds	12	Cyprus CDS
13	Madrid SE general	13	Netherlands bonds	13	Iceland CDS
14	Malta SE MSE	14	Norway bonds	14	Italy CDS
15	MDAX Frankfurt	15	Portugal bonds	15	Malta CDS
16	OMX Copenhagen	16	Spain bonds	16	Portugal CDS
17	OMX Helsinki	17	Sweden bonds	17	UK CDS
18	OMX Iceland all share	18	Switzerland bonds	18	Finland CDS
19	OMX Stockholm	19	US bonds		
20	Oslo exchange all share				
21	Portugal PSI all-share				
22	Swiss market				

Data and Methodology

Our data consists in two sets of financial instruments traded on the international markets: on one hand we are covering the dynamics of the equity indices, sovereign bonds with 5 year maturity and sovereign CDS contracts for a series of developed markets and on the other hand we investigate the dynamics of the same type of assets (equity indices, sovereign bonds and CDS contracts) for the Eastern European financial markets.

The data in Table 1 are used for the period January 2008 until July 2015, representing a set of 1977 log-returns for each asset. Figure 1 shows the boxplots for each asset and we can notice the fact that the distributions tend to be similar for each asset class, with average log-returns around the level of zero and with similar standard deviations especially for the equity log returns. The standard deviations of the log-returns for the bond markets are larger especially due to the low levels of bond values, while the CDS log-returns show a large level of volatility, but relatively similar across the countries covered by our analysis.

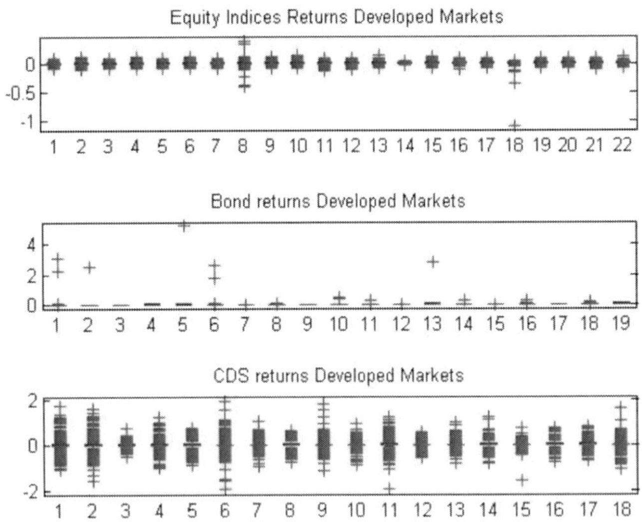

Source: Authors' computation.

Figure 1. The distributions of the log-returns for the assets in the Developed financial markets[1].

[1] The numbers in the Ox axis correspond to the numbers allocated to the assets in Table 1.

Table 2. The instruments for the Eastern European financial markets

Equity Indices		Sovereign Bonds		Sovereign CDS	
1	ATHEX composite	1	Bulgaria bond	1	Czech republic CDS
2	Budapest	2	Hungary bond	2	Bulgaria CDS
3	Bulgaria SE SOFIX	3	Lithuania bond	3	Croatia CDS
4	Croatia CROBEX	4	Poland bond	4	Estonia CDS
5	Cyprus general	5	Romania bond	5	Hungary CDS
6	OMX Riga	6	Slovakia bond	6	Latvia CDS
7	OMX Tallinn	7	Czech rep bond	7	Lithuania CDS
8	OMX Vilnius	8	Russian Fed bond	8	Poland CDS
9	Prague SE PX	9		9	Serbia CDS
10	Romania BET			10	Slovenia CDS
11	Russia RTS index			11	Romania CDS
12	Slovakia SAX 16			12	Russia CDS
13	Slovenian blue chip			13	Slovakia CDS
14	Warsaw general index			14	Ukraine CDS

The financial assets considered for the Central and Eastern European markets are presented in Table 2 above. The data that we use cover the same period as in the case of the assets of the developed financial markets, i.e., 1977 daily log-returns for the time span between January 2008 and July 2015.

A brief presentation of the distribution of the log-returns for the CEE financial markets is produced in Figure 2, in which we can observe the boxplots of these time variables. We notice the same type of variation for each asset class, as in the case of the developed markets. At every moment the series exhibit approximately the same mean around zero and larger volatilities in the case of the log-returns for the Russia RTS Index and the Cyprus stock index on one hand, and for the Poland CDS, Russia CDS and Slovakia CDS on the other hand.

The events that we took into account were the ones related to two types of monetary decisions by the Federal Open Market Committee on the US economy: the quantitative easing decisions and the tapering decisions. The following table shows the dates when these decisions were made:

Table 3. The dates for the event-study analysis

Quantitative Easing events	Tapering events
08/10/2010	22/05/2013
08/27/2010	03/06/2013
09/21/2010	19/06/2013
10/12/2010	31/07/2013
10/15/2010	18/09/2013
11/03/2010	30/10/2013
06/22/2011	18/12/2013
09/21/2011	29/01/2014
06/20/2012	19/03/2014
08/22/2012	30/04/2014
09/13/2012	18/06/2014
12/12/2012	30/07/2014
	17/09/2014
	29/10/2014

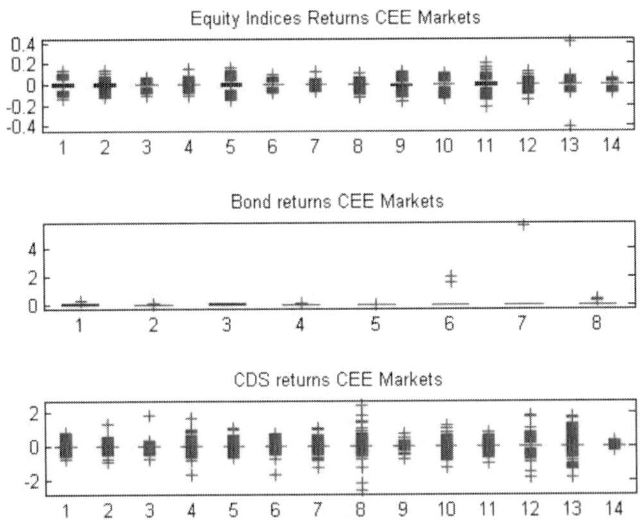

Source: Authors' computation.

Figure 2. The distributions of the log-returns for the assets in the CEE financial markets[2].

[2] The numbers in the Ox axis correspond to the numbers allocated to the assets in Table 2.

The first step of our analysis consists in the application of the Markov switching model with two states for the dynamics of the log-returns for each series of equities, bonds and CDS contracts respectively. We used the algorithm for the univariate series and we identified the changes for each asset class.

Once the transition probabilities were estimated, we computed the probabilities for the series of returns to be either in state 1 or in state 2, as marginal probabilities of the set of transition probabilities for each moment in time. We used the threshold of 90% as a level large enough to consider that there is enough evidence for the log-returns to behave, for instance, as in state 1 when the probability to be in state 1 is larger than 90%. Once we succeed to do the same for both of the states, we took into account the moments when there is enough evidence for the log-returns to move from one state to the other.

Figure 3 shows three heat maps for the dynamics of the changes between the two states for each asset class and for the whole sample in our analysis (the Ox axis contains the time span from January 2008 to July 2015). We can notice that there are a few instruments that tend to shift very often and there are others that change regimes rather seldom. Most of the changes that could be identified in a simultaneous manner are present especially in the case of the equity index returns (the tendency to notice vertical lines signals common regime shifts).

Once the shifts were identified (using the threshold of 90% for the transition probabilities) we investigated the tendency of each group of assets to exhibit regime shifts in the same time. Figure 4 shows the histograms of the shifts that were produced independently (the 0 column of the histograms), in two cases (column 1), three cases (column 2) and so on. We can observe that we have situations in which there were even 21 assets that changed in the same time for the equity indices, a tendency to move together for the bond returns (an average of 16 assets that changed in the same time) and not more than 5 sovereign assets that changed in the same time.

The moments in which we identified at least 2 assets that changed their regimes in the same time are presented in Figure 5. We notice that the CDS log-returns tend to show fewer changes that happened in the same time (also due to the fact that these financial instruments are more stable, their probabilities to stay in a certain state given that the log-returns are in that state are larger than the ones that denote changes from one state to another), followed by the equity indices log-returns, while the bonds exhibit a lot of regime switches.

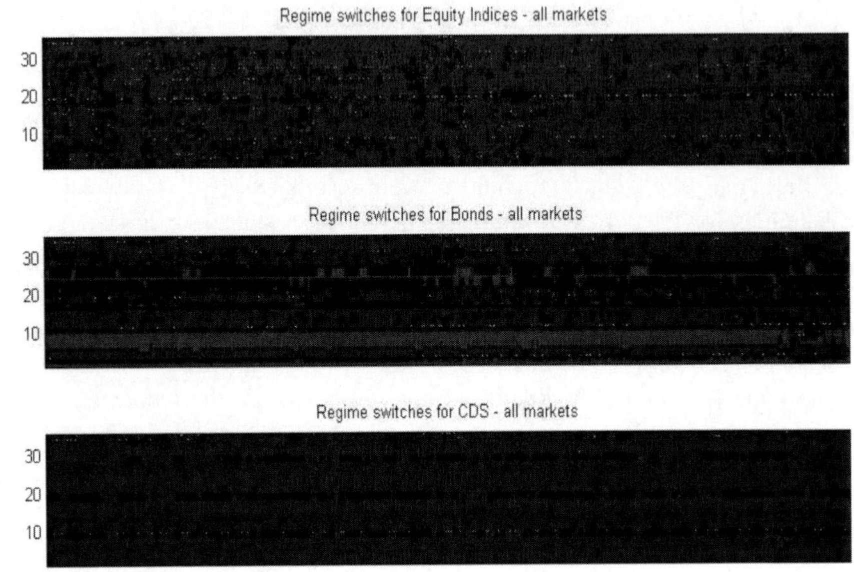

Source: Authors' computation.

Figure 3. Heat maps of regime shifts for each asset class.

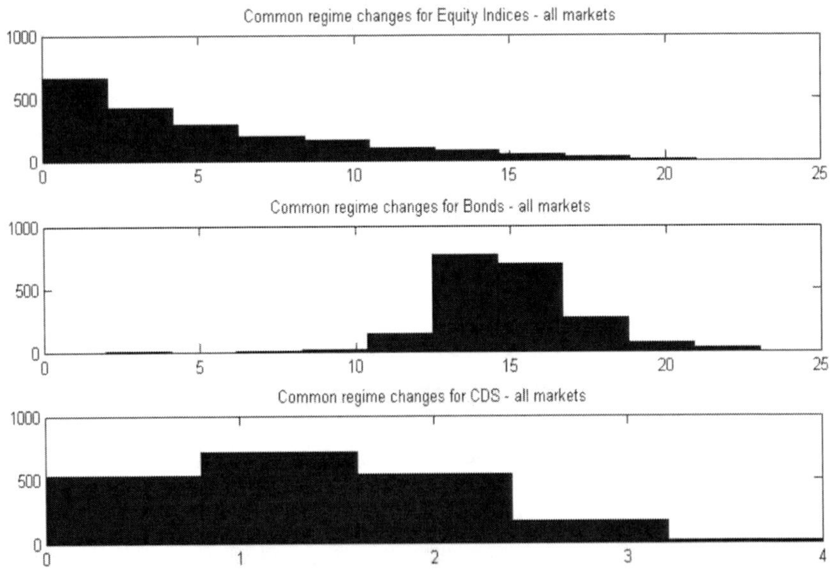

Source: Authors' computation.

Figure 4. Histograms of regime shifts for financial instruments for all markets.

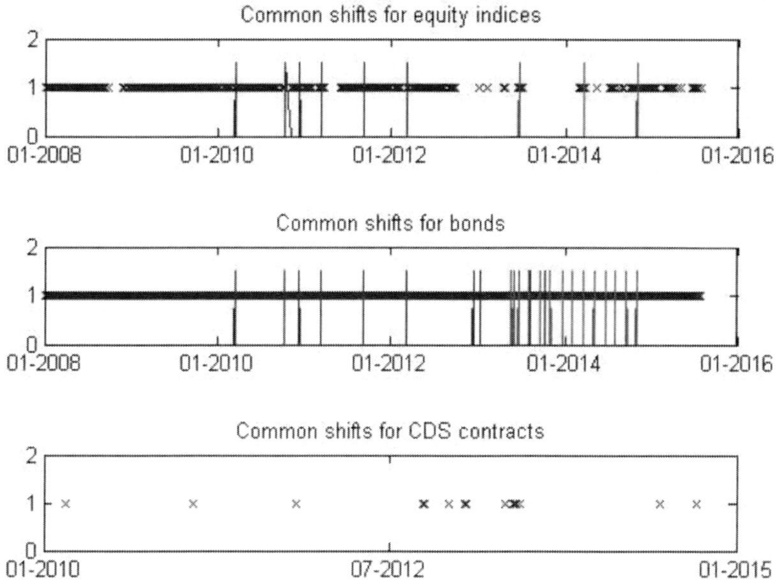

Source: Authors' computation.

Figure 5. The time span of moments with common shifts for each asset class.

In the same figure, the blue columns represent the moments when the quantitative easing decisions were made, while the red columns notify the days in which the tapering decisions were made. The chart only shows those quantitative easing and tapering moments in which we also identified a shift in the regimes using the Markov switching algorithm. Therefore, we notice that only six quantitative easing events were matched with moments of regime shifts, and only three tapering events happened in the same time with a regime shifts in the equity indices. We can also see that no such monetary decision was matched with a regime shift for the CDS market. As far as the bonds are concerned, we observe that ten of the quantitative easing moments were matched with regime shifts and all the tapering moments were matched with regime changing moments.

The next step of our investigation consisted in the employment of an event-study analysis for the changes in the volatilities of the three types of assets and for each set of markets (i.e., developed and non-developed) at the moments of the release of the quantitative easing and tapering announcements. The procedure consists in the fitting of a set of volatility models from the GARCH class that are calibrated for a sample of 500 days previous to the time of the event and a window of 21 days centered on each event (ten days before the event and ten days after that moment). The set of models is the following: GARCH(1,1), EGARCH(1,1), ZARCH(1,1), APARCH(1,1), GJR-GARCH (1,1) and NAGARCH(1,1), with the following specifications:

Model	Specification
GARCH	$\sigma_t^2 = \alpha_0 + \sum_{i=1}^{m} \alpha_i a_{t-i}^2 + \sum_{j=1}^{s} \beta_j \sigma_{t-j}^2$ where $\alpha_0 > 0, \alpha_i \geq 0, \beta_j \geq 0$ and $\sum_{i=1}^{\max(m,s)} (\alpha_i + \beta_i) < 1$
EGARCH	yt $= \mu + a_t,\ a_t = \sigma_t \epsilon_t$ $$\log \sigma_t^2 = \omega + \sum_{i=1}^{m} \beta_i \log \sigma_{t-i}^2 + \sum_{j=1}^{s} \alpha_j \left[\frac{\lvert a_{t-j} \rvert}{\sigma_{t-j}} - E\left(\frac{\lvert a_{t-j} \rvert}{\sigma_{t-j}} \right) \right] + \sum_{j=1}^{s} \gamma_j \left(\frac{a_{t-j}}{\sigma_{t-j}} \right)$$
ZARCH	yt $= \mu + a_t,\ a_t = \sigma_t \epsilon_t, \sigma_t = \omega + \sum_{i=1}^{m} \beta_i \sigma_{t-i} + \sum_{j=1}^{s} (\alpha_j a_{t-j}^{+} + \gamma_j \lvert a_{t-j}^{-} \rvert)$ where: $a^{+} = \max(a,0)\ and\ a^{-} = \min(a,0)$
A-PARCH	yt $= \mu + a_t,\ a_t = \sigma_t \epsilon_t, \sigma_t^{\delta} = \omega + \sum_{i=1}^{m} \beta_i \sigma_{t-i}^{\delta} + \sum_{j=1}^{s} \alpha_j (\lvert a_{t-j} \rvert - \gamma_j a_{t-j})^{\delta}$ where: $\omega > 0, \delta \geq 0, \beta_i \geq 0, \alpha_j \geq 0, -1 < \gamma_j < 1$
GARCH – GJR	yt $= \mu + a_t,\ a_t = \sigma_t \epsilon_t, \sigma_t^2 = \omega + \sum_{i=1}^{m} \beta_i \sigma_{t-i}^2 + \sum_{j=1}^{s} \alpha_j a_{t-j}^2 + \sum_{j=1}^{s} \gamma_j I_{t-j} a_{t-j}^2$
NAGARCH	$\sigma_{t+1}^2 = \omega + \alpha R_t^2 + \beta'^{\sigma_t^2} - 2\alpha\delta z_t \sigma_t^2$, where $\beta' \equiv \beta + \alpha\delta^2 > \beta'\ in\ the\ case\ in\ which\ \alpha > 0$

For each asset in our sample and for each event we used the sample of 500 returns before the - 10 day of the event to fit each of the six types of volatility models. These models were used to build a forecast for the dynamics of the volatility during the event window (a forecast for the next 21 days around the event). We took into account the variances produced by the volatility models in the last 20 days before the day - 10 of the event window (i.e., in the last 20 days of the fitting interval), we computed deviations from the squared returns to these variances and we calculated the average of their absolute values.

For the time interval of 21 days around each event we compared the forecasts for the variances produced by each volatility model with the squared returns realized inside this window. We considered that we have identified a significant reaction in the variance at a certain time moment inside the window if the deviation was larger than twice the average deviation computed for the last 20 days before the event window, i.e., before the day - 10, inside the fitting interval.

RESULTS

This section provides a set of results that summarize the computations described previously. We divided these analysis into representations that cover the volatility reaction of the quantitative easing decisions and separately of the tapering decisions, for each asset type and for each group of countries (developed and Central and Eastern European financial markets).

In the end we also showed some results concerning the differences in the reactions perceived by the two types of financial markets with respect to each set of events.

Figure 6 shows the percentage of significant situations in which each type of asset class reacted to the set of quantitative easing monetary decisions. In the Oy axis we show the 12 events, and on the Ox axis we have the results as computed according to each type of volatility model. The Oz axis shows the proportion of significant reactions that we could observe for each event inside the 21 days around the event. A zero bar signals a situation in which none of the squared returns realized inside an interval covering day - 2 to day + 2 (a five day interval) exceeded twice the level of average deviations produced by the respective volatility model in the last 20 days before the day -10. On the contrary, a bar with the size of 1 would signify the fact that all the deviations of squared returns less forecasted variances inside this interval (from day - 2 to day + 2) exceeded twice the average deviation.

We notice more reactions in the first three quantitative easing events for the equity indices and even more for the bond log-returns. The CDSs reacted more in the last part of the event, i.e., the events from 2012. With very few exceptions the same results can be observed for all the volatility models.

A larger percentage of significant situations were observed for the tapering events for all the asset classes. The largest reactions were perceived in the case of the equity indices and also we observed important reactions for the bond returns. The CDS returns reacted mainly in the first part of the year 2013 and to a lower extend by the end of 2014.

The Central and Eastern European financial markets showed significant reactions with respect to the quantitative easing events in the case of stock indices and sovereign bonds. The most important part was the one towards the end of the sample, i.e., from 2012. The CDS market reacted mostly at the beginning of the set of events and also by its end, before the set of tapering events. Again, we can observe that the reactions are approximately similar when compared across model types. The reactions to these events for a set of assets belonging to the CEE financial markets can be considered as evidence in favor of market integration.

The tapering events seem to have produced larger and more significant reactions for the CEE financial markets for all the events in our analysis. We notice in Figure 9 an approximate same pattern in which the CDS log-returns reacted to a larger extent to these events than in the case of the quantitative easing. The tapering could be considered as a phenomenon that converted the investments from the developed markets towards the emerging markets, which could generate larger returns and different investment opportunities. Both the bonds and the equity indices returns reacted heavily to almost all the events taken into account.

Figures 10 and 11 show the differences in the significance for the two types of financial markets and reveal the possible different manner for the investors in these two markets to react to the same type of phenomenon. A positive bar shows a reaction that is larger in the case of the developed markets than in the case of the CEE markets.

From this perspective, Figure 10 shows these differences for the case of the quantitative easing events and for each asset class. We notice that the developed markets exhibited larger reactions to these events than the CEE markets, especially in the first part of the QE events (i.e., in 2010). The CEE markets showed larger reactions only in the case of the bond returns and especially at the end of the quantitative easing moments, which could be considered as a prelude for the initiation of the tapering events.

The differences between the significance situations for the tapering events show that most of the times the reactions were larger in the case of the developed markets for the equity indices. In addition to this we observe similar effects for the bond and larger ones for the CEE markets in the case of CDS returns, especially for the events at the end of 2013 and beginning of 2014. The positive and negative differences show that these markets tend to be integrated since the differences do not show a very clear pattern. If we consider these events as being part of the same class (i.e., we do not differentiate between the various specifics of each tapering event) then the reactions are rather similar for the developed and CEE markets, which could be considered as evidence of market integration.

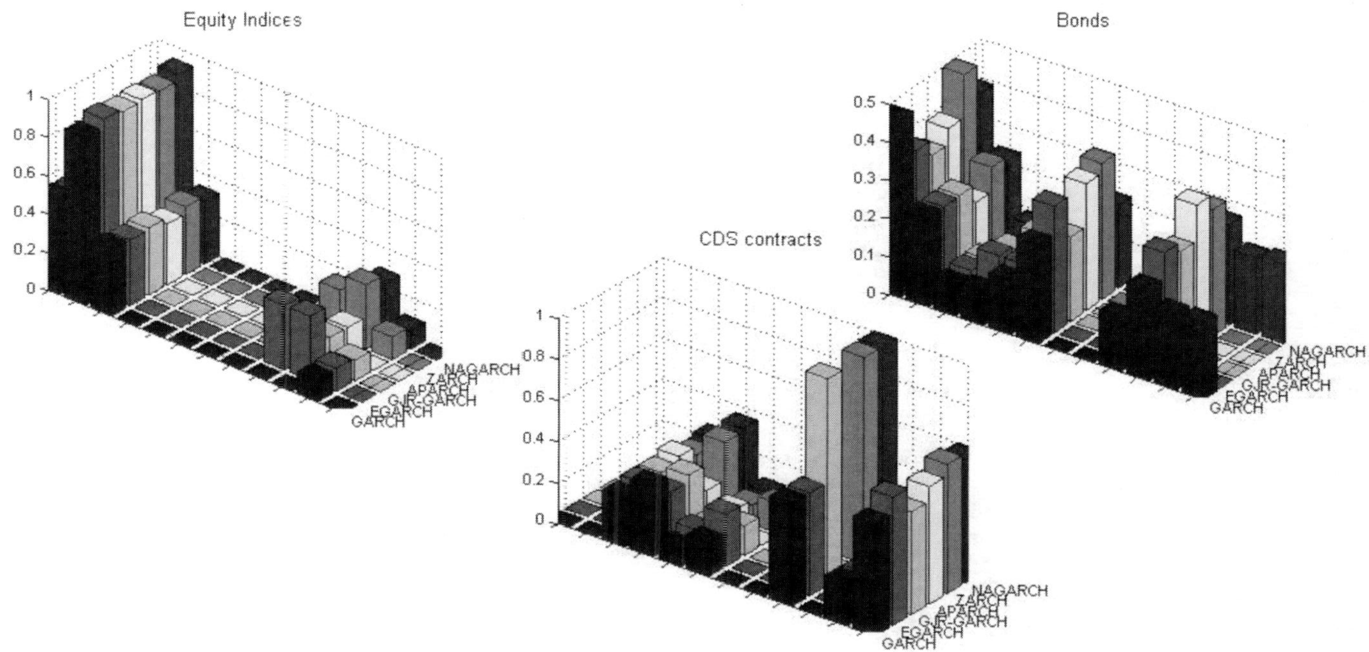

Source: Authors' computation.

Figure 6. Percentage of significance of developed markets for Quantitative Easing decisions.

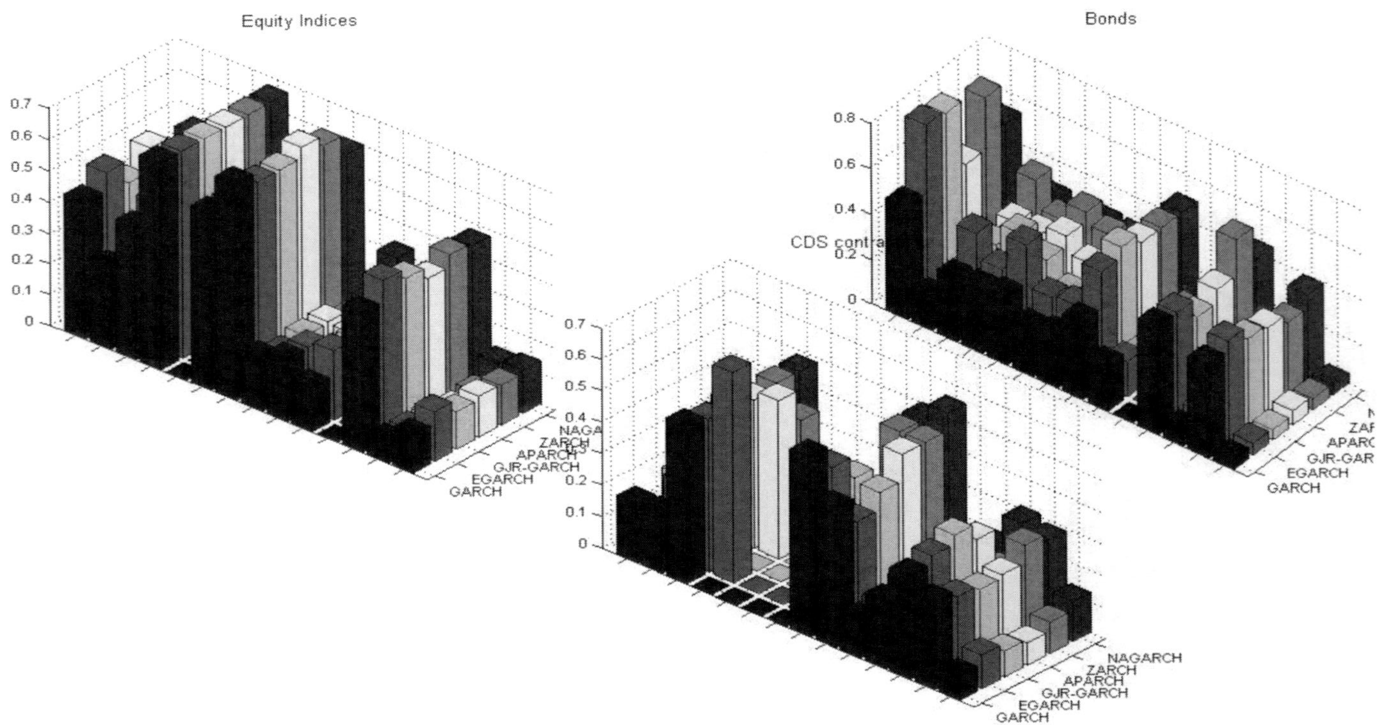

Source: Authors' computation.

Figure 7. Percentage of significance of developed markets for tapering decisions.

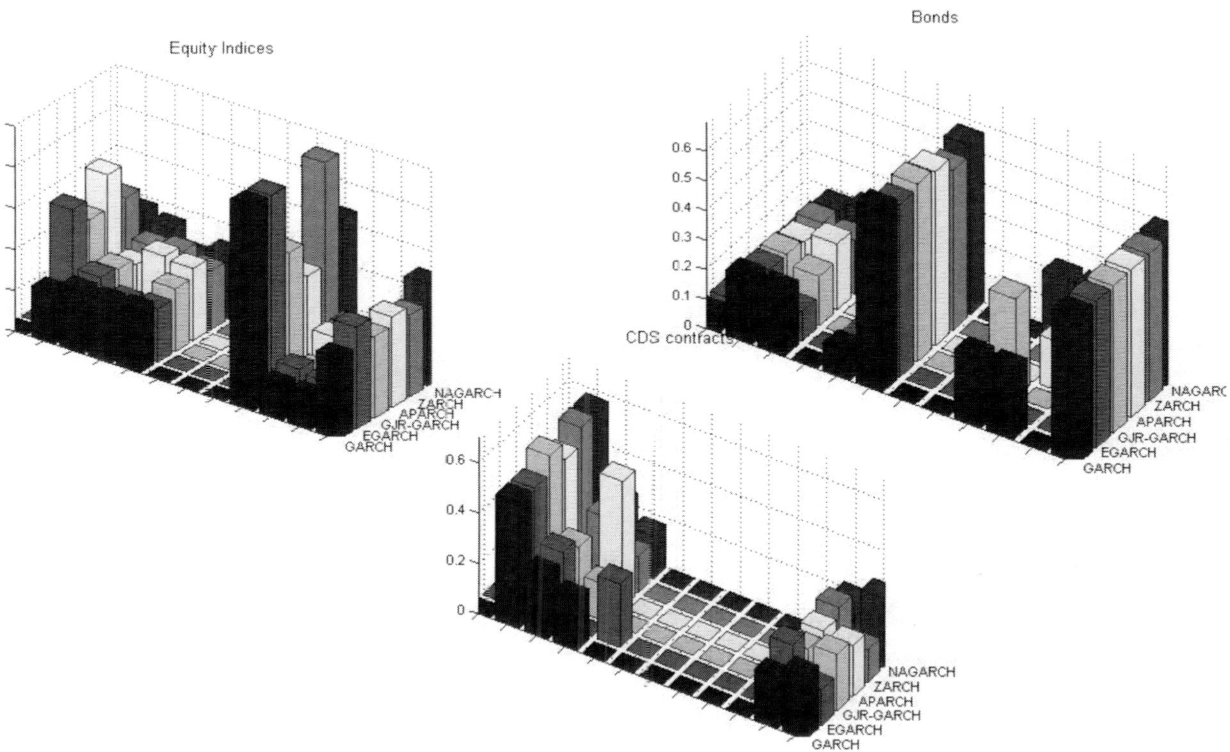

Source: Authors' computation.

Figure 8. Percentage of significance of CEE markets for Quantitative Easing decisions.

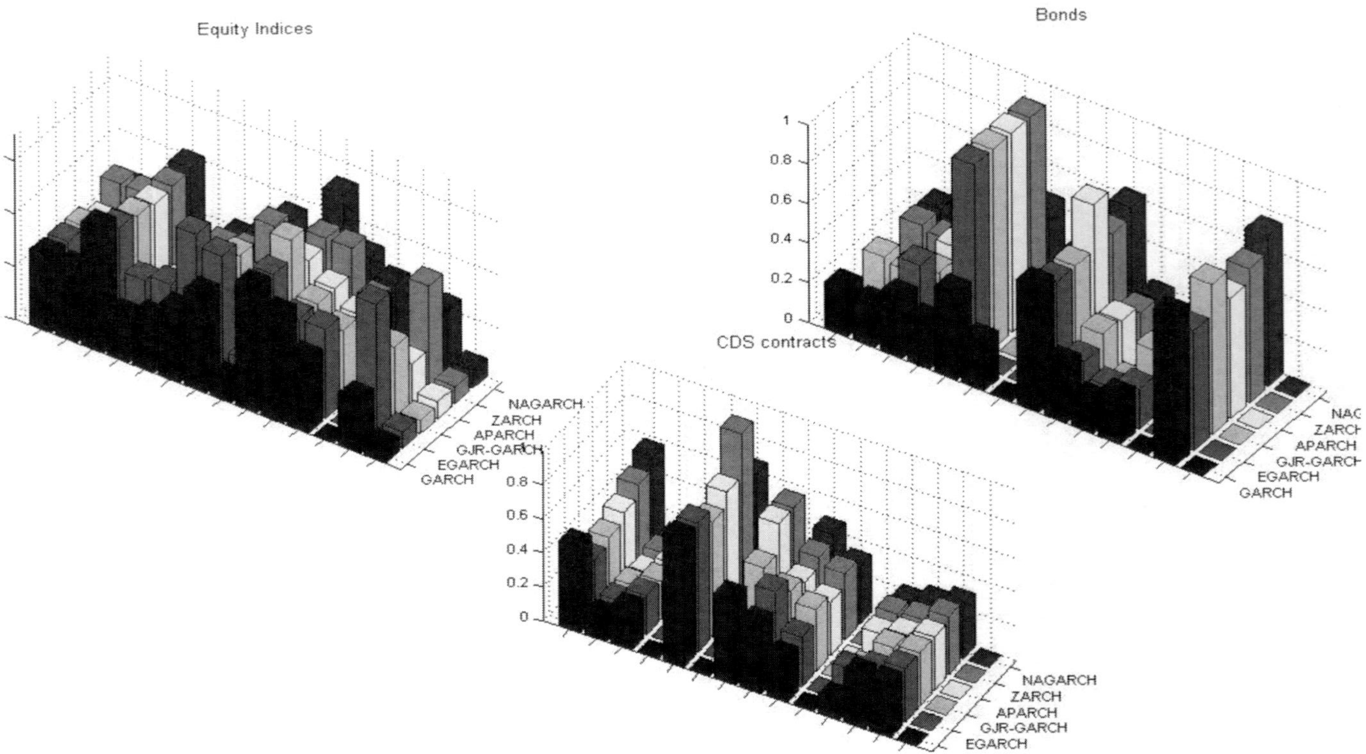

Source: Authors' computation.

Figure 9. Percentage of significance of CEE markets for Tapering decisions.

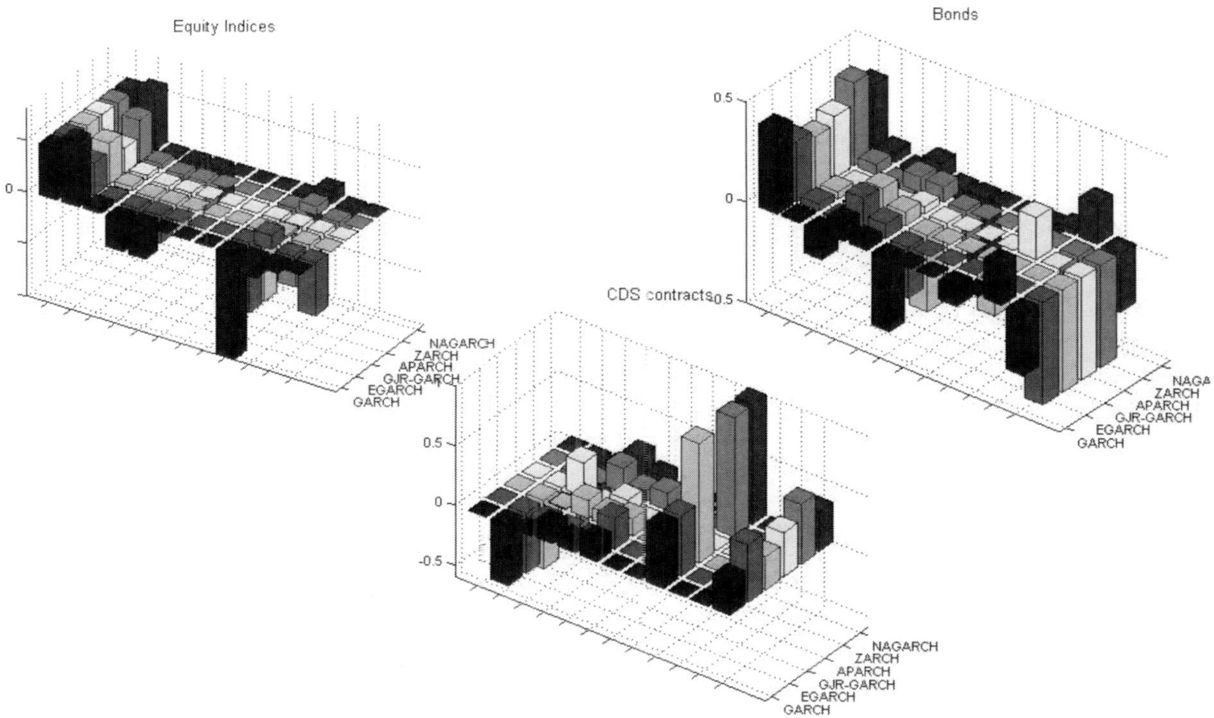

Source: Authors' computation.

Figure 10. Differences in significance between developed and CEE instruments for Quantitative Easing events.

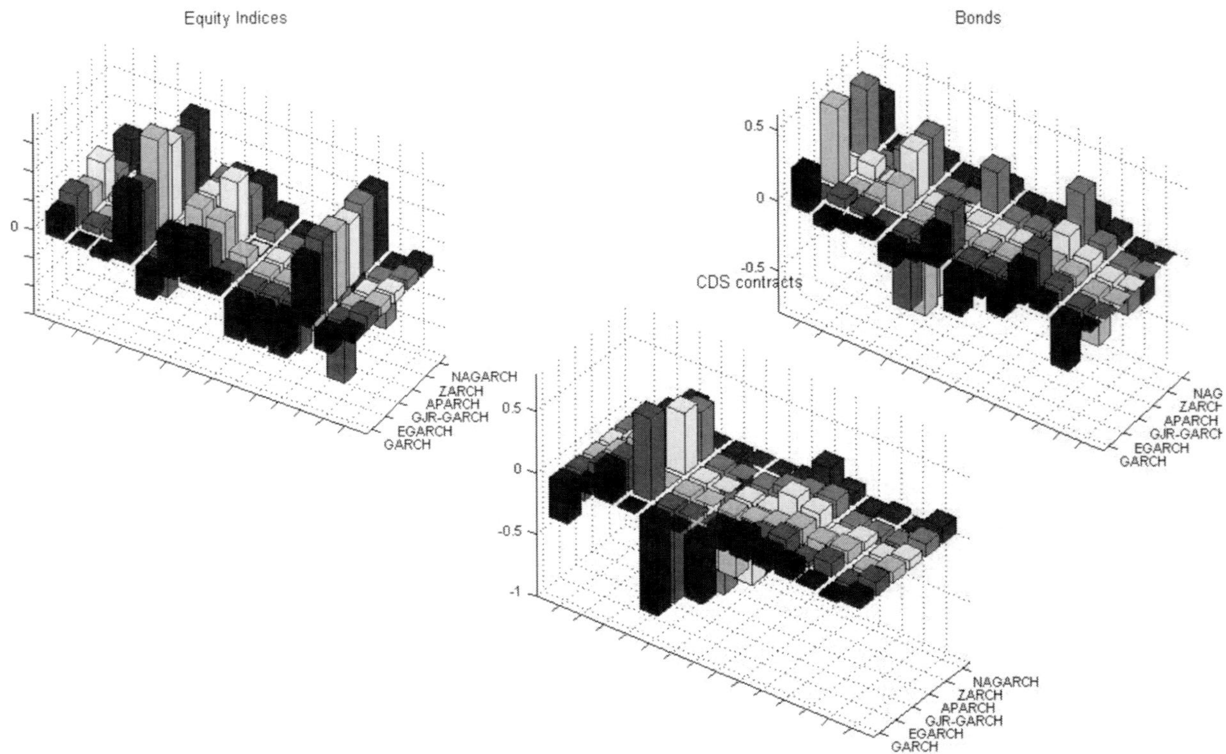

Source: Authors' computation.

Figure 11. Differences in significance between developed and CEE instruments for Tapering events.

CONCLUSION

Our analysis consisted in the investigation of the impact of two types of macroeconomic monetary decisions made by the Federal Open Market Committee on various types of assets and two different financial markets – a set of developed markets and Central and Eastern European markets. The investigation consisted in two types of analyses – one that assumed the identification of the moments when the log-returns of the financial assets under analysis exhibited regime shifts in their dynamics and another one that dealt with the employment of an event-study methodology to identify the volatility reaction of all the assets. According to the first set of analyses we noticed that the regime shifts take place in the case of the events under our analysis both for the equity indices and for the bonds. The CDS log-returns did not exhibit a lot of regime shifts when compared to the other types of assets. As far as the event study is concerned, we found evidence in favor of significant reactions both for the developed and CEE markets for each asset class. These were considered as important evidence in favor of financial market integration of the CEE markets. The volatility reactions to tapering events were generally larger than the reactions to the quantitative easing events, mostly for equity indices and bonds.

REFERENCES

Aizenman, Joshua, Mahir Binici, and Michael M. Hutchison. 2014. "The Transmission of Federal Reserve Tapering News to Emerging Financial Markets," *NBER Working Pape*r 19980: doi:10.3386/w19980.

Albu, Lucian Liviu, Radu Lupu, Adrian Cantemir Calin, and Oana Cristina Popovici. 2014a. "Estimating the Impact of Quantitative Easing on Credit and Risk Through an ARMA – GARH Model." *The Romanian Journal of Economic Forecasting* vol. XVII: 39-50.

Albu, Lucian Liviu, Radu Lupu, Adrian Cantemir Calin, and Oana Cristina Popovici. 2014b. "The effect of ECB's Quantitative Easing on Credit Default Swap Instruments in Central and Eastern Europe," *Procedia Economics and Finance* 8: 122-128.

Bernanke, Ben S., Vincent R. Reinhart, and Brian P. Sack. 2004. "Monetary policy alternatives at the zero bound: An empirical assessment," *Brookings Papers on Economic Activity* 35(2): 1-100.

Bowman David, Fang Cai, Sally Davies, and Steven Kamin. 2015. "Quantitative easing and bank lending: Evidence from Japan." *Journal of International Money and Finance* 57: 15-30.

Bridges Jonathan, Ryland Thomas. 2012. "The impact of QE on the UK economy - some supportive monetarist arithmetic." *Bank of England Working Pape*r 442.

Călin, Adrian Cantemir. 2015 a. *Impactul deciziilor de politică monetară de stimulare a economiei asupra piețelor financiare international* (The impact of monetary policy decisions to stimulate the economy on the international financial markets). Craiova: Sitech Publishing House.

Călin, Adrian Cantemir. 2015 b. "Eloquence is The Key – the Impact of Monetary Policy Speeches on Exchange Rate Volatility," *The Romanian Economic Journal* 56: 3-18.

Călin, Adrian Cantemir. 2015 c. "The Effects of the Federal Reserve's Tapering Announcement on the US Real Estate Market," *Financial studies* 19(3): 79-90.

Cherubini, Umberto, and Roberto Violi. 2015. "Government Bonds Ammunitions for the ECB Quantitative Easing," doi: 10.13140/RG.2. 1.4416.4008.

D'Amico, Stefania, and Thomas B. 2010. "Flow and Stock Effects of Large-Scale Treasury Purchases," *Federal Reserve Board, Finance and Economics Discussion Series.*

D'Amico, Stefania, English William, David Lopez-Salido, and Edward Nelson. 2012. "The Federal Reserve's Large-Scale Asset Purchase Programs: Rationale and Effects," *Working Paper*, Federal Reserve Board: 1-58.

Dale, Spencer. 2010. 'QE – one year on.' Paper presented at the CIMF and MMF Research Group Conference "New Instruments of Monetary Policy: The Challenges," Cambridge, March 12.

de Grawe, Paul, and Ji Yuemeni. 2015. "Quantitative Easing in the Eurozone. It's Possible without Fiscal Transfers," *Cesifo Area Conference on Macro*, Money and International Finance.

Doh, Taeyoung. 2010. "The Efficacy of Large-Scale Asset Purchases at the Zero Lower Bound," *Federal Reserve Bank of Kansas City Economic Review.*

Eichengreen, Barry, and Poonam Gupta. 2013. "Tapering talk: the impact of expectations of Reduced Federal Reserve security purchases on emerging markets," *unpublished*, University of Berkeley.

Fawley, Brett W., and Christopher Neely. 2013. "Four Stories of Quantitative Easing," *Federal Reserve Bank of St. Louis Review* 95(1): 51-88.

Gagnon, Joseph, Matthew Raskin, Julie Remache, and Brian Sack. 2011. "The Financial Market Effects of the Federal Reserve's Large-Scale Asset Purchases," *International Journal of Central Banking* 7: 3-43.

Gertler, Mark, and Peter Karadi. 2012. "QE 1 vs. 2 vs. 3...A Framework for Analyzing Large Scale Asset Purchases as a Monetary Policy Tool," *International Journal of Central Banking* 9 S1: 5-53.

Hayashi, Fumio, and Junko Koeda. 2014. "Exiting from QE," *CARF F-Series CARF-F-322, Center for Advanced Research in Finance, Faculty of Economics*, University of Tokyo 12.

Joyce, Michael, Matthew Tong, and Robert Woods. 2011. "The United Kingdom's quantitative easing policy: design, operation and impact," *Quarterly Bulletin* Q3 18.

Joyce, Michael A.S., Ana Lasaosa, Ibrahim Stevens, and Matthew Tong. 2011. "The financial market impact of quantitative easing in the United Kingdom," *International Journal of Central Banking* 7(3): 113-162.

Joyce, Michael A.S., Marco Spaltro. 2014. "Quantitative Easing and Bank Lending: a Panel Data Approach," *Working Paper* No. 504 for The Bank of England.

Kapetanios, George, Haroon Mumtaz, Ibrahim Stevens, and Konstantinos Theodoridis. 2012. "Assessing the Economy-wide Effects of Quantitative Easing," *The Economic Journal* 15: 316-347.

Kimura, Takeshi, and David Small. 2004. "Quantitative Monetary Easing and Risk in Financial Asset Markets," *Finance and Economics Discussion Series Divisions of Research and Statistics and Monetary Affairs Federal Reserve Board*, Washington, D.C.

Kimura, Takeshi, and Jouchi Nakajima. 2013. "Identifying Conventional and Unconventional Monetary Policy Shocks: A Latent Threshold Approach," mimeo, April.

Krishnamurthy, Arvind, and Annette Vissing-Jorgensen. 2013. "The ins and outs of LSAPs," *Federal Reserve Bank of Kansas City, Proceedings-Economic Policy Symposium-Jackson Hole.*

Li, Canlin, and Min Wei. 2013. "Term Structure Modeling with Supply Factors and the Federal Reserve's Large-Scale Asset Purchase Programs," *International Journal of Central Banking* 9(1): 1-39.

Lupu, Radu, and Adrian Cantemir Calin. 2014. "To QE or not to QE. The Japanese Experience," *Hyperion Economic Journal* 2(2): 3-10.

Lupu, Radu, and Adrian Cantemir Calin. 2014 b. "Co-movements of Regime Shifts in GBP currency pairs around BOE Quantitative Easing Announcements," *Financial Studies* 18(3): 89-101.

Lyonnet, Victor, and Richard Werner. 2012. "Lessons from the Bank of England on 'quantitative easing' and other 'unconventional' monetary policies," [in special issue: Banking and the Economy] *International Review of Financial Analysis* 25: 94-105.

Meier, Andre. 2009. "Panacea, curse, or nonevent? Unconventional monetary policy in the United Kingdom," *International Monetary Fund, Working Paper No. 09/163*, Aug.

Oda, Nobuyuki, and Kazuo Ueda. 2005. "The effects of the Bank of Japan's zero interest rate commitment and quantitative monetary easing on the yield curve: A macro-finance approach," Tokyo: *Bank of Japan Working Paper No. 5-E-6*, April.

Peersman, Geert. 2011. "Macroeconomic Effects of Unconventional Monetary Policy in the Euro Area," *European Central bank Working Paper NO 1397*.

Shibamoto, Masahiko, and Minoru Tachibana. 2014. "The Effect of Unconventional Monetary Policy on the Macro Economy: Evidence from Japan's Quantitative Easing Policy Period," *Kobe University, Discussion Paper*.

Shiratsuka, Shigenori. 2010. "Size and Composition of the Central Bank Balance Sheet: Revisiting Japanfs Experience of the Quantitative Easing Policy," *Monetary and Economic Studies, Institute for Monetary and Economic Studies, Bank of Japan* 28: 79-106.

Sosvilla-Riveroa, Simon, and Natalia Fernández-Fernández. 2015. "Unconventional monetary policy and the dollar–euro exchange rate: first results from time-series analysis," *Applied Economics Letters*, doi:10. 1080/13504851.2015.1102841.

SteeleY, James M. 2015. "The side effects of quantitative easing: Evidence from the UK bond market," *Journal of International Money and Finance* 51: 303-336.

Szczerbowicz, Urszula. 2014. "The ECB's Unconventional Monetary Policies: Have they lowered market borrowing costs for banks and governments?" *RIETI Discussion Paper Series 14-E-008*.

Tachibana, Minoru. 2015. "Comparing the Macroeconomic Effects of Conventional and Unconventional Monetary Policy in Japan," *Osaka Prefecture University, Discussion Paper New Series* No. 2015-3.

Ugai, Hiroshi. 2007. "Effects of the Quantitative Easing Policy: A Survey of Empirical Analyses," *Monetary and Economic Studies*, Institute for Monetary and Economic Studies, Bank of Japan 25(1): 1-48.

In: Non-Linear Modeling
Editors: L. Liviu Albu and P. Caraiani
ISBN: 978-1-63484-932-6

Chapter 3

POSITIONING EASTERN EUROPEAN ECONOMIES IN THE INTERNATIONAL FINANCE NETWORK

***Lucian Liviu Albu**, *Radu Lupu*† and *Crina Pungulescu*‡**
Institute for Economic Forecasting, Bucharest, Romania

PACS: 05.45-a, 52.35.Mw, 96.50.Fm

Keywords: European Union, Eastern Europe, International Financial Networks, Financial Crisis

JEL Subject Classification: F36, G11, G15

1. Introduction

The recent crisis has prompted investigation of the web of financial interactions that encompass virtually all the world. While ever increasing connections seem to be a matter of course, it is undecided whether this improves risk sharing or exposure to contagion. Allen and Gale [2000] link contagion with a state of incomplete market structure and the model of Babus [2007] implies a that a connectivity threshold exists, above which contagion does not occur. At the same time, Battiston et al. [2012] warn that "a financial network can be most resilient

*E-mail address: albul@ipe.ro.
†E-mail address: radu.lupu@rei.ase.ro.
‡E-mail address: crina_pungulescu@ipe.ro (Corresponding author).

for intermediate levels of risk diversification, and not when this is maximal, as generally thought so far." While the debate on the optimal level of connectivity is ongoing, the empirical analysis of the state and evolution of individual and regional connectivity is a necessary first step. Allen and Babus [2009] argue that representing financial systems as networks of nodes and links helps understanding their process of formation and effects on stability, elements of particular policy interest. This chapter details and directs such analysis to the 11 East European members of the European Union (Bulgaria, Croatia, Czech Republic, Estonia, Hungary, Latvia, Lithuania, Poland, Romania, Slovak Republic and Slovenia).

The main aim of the chapter is to identify and characterize the position of the 11 East European countries (EEC) of interest in the international financial network, as well as its dynamics over the 2000s and especially during the peak of the financial crisis (2007-2008). Further individualized scrutiny is directed to their choice of investment partners and the eventual shifts spurred by the financial crisis with the objective to uncover testable hypotheses on the factors shaping international investments strategy in crisis.

The findings show that the EEC have become more connected over the period and some of the countries compare well with more developed markets. Their evolution mirrors global trends, for instance there is a visible crisis effect but it is less pronounced than the world average. At the same time, the region is clearly undergoing a process of development and change and its dynamics are far less stable than those of the European Union (EU) and the world as a whole. In more recent years, however a tendency of convergence is apparent. A more indepth exploration of the individual choices of investment partners identifies for each of the EEC a preferential relationship to one of its neighbours (Bulgaria - Greece, Czech Republic - Slovak Republic, Estonia - Finland, Hungary - Austria, Latvia - Estonia, Lithuania - Sweden, Poland - Germany, Romania - Bulgaria, Slovak Republic - Czech Republic, Slovenia - Austria) and invites further and more formal research into the roles played by economic and cultural factors in determining the EEC's portfolio choices. The extreme episode of the financial crisis provides the opportunity for testing the resiliency of such preferential relationships.

The remainder of the chapter is organized as follows. Section 2 describes the characteristics of the dataset and section 3 applies various indicators to position the EEC in the international financial network. Section 4 explores the individual choices of the EEC in terms of partners. Section 5 concludes and provides hypotheses for further research.

2. Data

This empirical analysis is made possible by the initiative of the International Monetary Fund (IMF) to conduct the Coordinated Portfolio Investment Survey (CPIS) in which an increasing number of economies and territories volunteer information about the geographical distribution of their foreign assets. The first trial was successfully conducted in 1997 and starting with 2001, the CPIS takes place every year. This chapter uses data on cross-border stocks and foreign direct investment for 12 years starting in 2001, relating to 80 source economies (reporting) and 241 destination economies (reported).

While the value-added in information brought about by such detailed statistics is substantial, it has to be noticed that several possible bias are in-built in this database. If for instance, country A uses a broker company in country B in order to ultimately invest in a third country C, the database will not allow us to uncover country A's holdings of country C's equity. Also, participating economies may (and do) on occasion choose to withhold information on the amounts of their holdings. This veils a part (more or less significant depending of the country in question) of the international financial network, restricting the discussions to the patterns present in the observable part of the network.

The clear unbalance (as most countries are represented only as destinations and thereby assumed implicitly as not investing abroad themselves) underestimates *de facto* the extent of the international network. However imperfect, the database does not cease to be a source of relevant information.

As the interest of this chapter is the dynamics and reactivity of foreign assets and liabilities in times of crisis, the variable of choice is foreign-held domestic equity (i.e. inward equity investment) and foreign equity assets (i.e. outward investments).

3. Network Indicators

This section investigates the position of the EEC in the international financial network by computing their individual scores at a set of network statistics [see Chinazzi et al., 2012, for a detailed description on network indicators].

3.1. Nodes and Links

Before zooming into the EEC's participation in the international financial network as represented by our dataset, a bird's eye view of the number of partners (either sources or destinations of investment) of each of the 241 countries included (see Figure 1), illustrates some basic aspects as well as the caveats discussed in the previous section. With the database necessarily unbalanced (only 80 countries report their investments including the remaining 161 countries only indirectly, when reported as destinations), a large number of non-reported links are assumed non-existent. Therefore, the network on which we have information, where 65% of the countries appear to have less than average number of partners (i.e. 26 in 2012) understates the actual fact. A further caveat refers to interpreting evolutions, as some of our countries of interest start reporting their investments only in recent years (Latvia in 2006, Lithuania and Slovenia in 2009), which causes the statistic of overall number of counterparties (i.e. sources and destinations) to (artificially) spike in those years. Croatia has not yet started to report its foreign holdings, which implicitly underestimates its position in the network. Nonetheless, a pattern emerges clearly and EEC appear to be increasing their interconnectedness, albeit at different speeds.

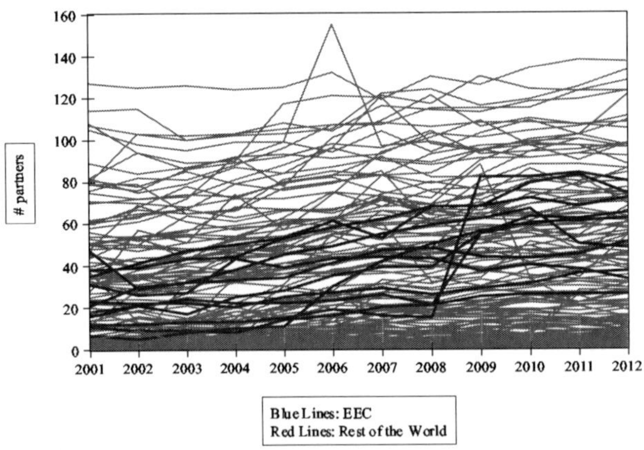

Figure 1. Number of Partners: All Countries. This figure shows the total number of partners (in both inward and outward equity investments) of the 11 EEC (identified by blue lines) and the remaining 230 countries covered by the dataset (red lines) over the period 2001 to 2012.

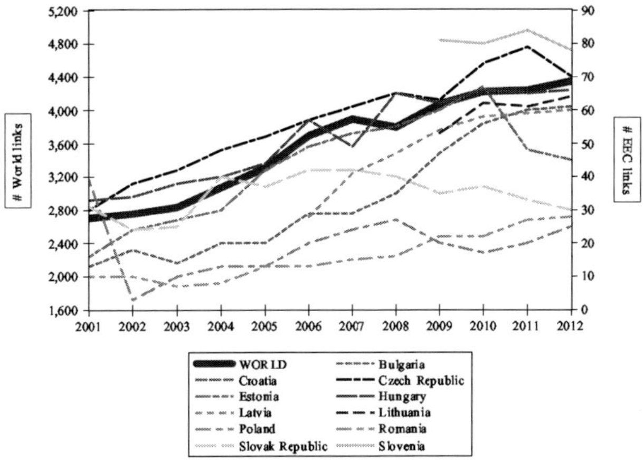

Figure 2. Number Outward Financial Links. This figure shows the number of outward financial links (i.e. where the countries represented are seen as sources of investment) of EEC as well as the world total over the period 2001 to 2012.

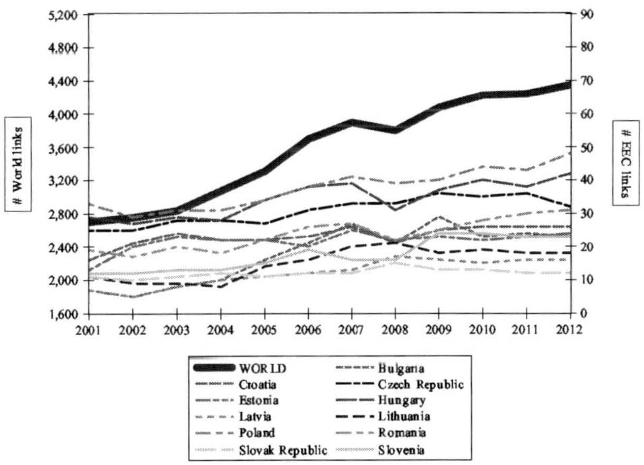

Figure 3. Number of Inward Financial Links. This figure shows the number of inward financial links (i.e. where the countries represented are seen as destinations of investment) of EEC as well as the world total over the period 2001 to 2012.

Assuming a maximum of 241 nodes in the financial network (given by the number of destination economies covered by the dataset), a complete structure would have 28920 of outward (i.e. investing abroad) and inward (i.e. receiving foreign investment) links. Figure 2 takes the EEC as sources of investment and illustrates the dynamics of their number of outward links (comparing it to the world total). While the crisis affects visibly the international financial network, with the number of global links having temporarily decreased in 2008, some of the EEC managed to increase the number of their destinations throughout the sample (notably Bulgaria and Latvia) while other appear to have decisively dropped connections (such as Estonia and the Slovak Republic for instance). Figure 3 shows the evolution of the number of inward links present in our database (world total as well as individual EEC). Stability in number of links is the common factor when it comes to Eastern Europe as a destination of investment, with all countries showing flatter slopes than that of the global links. Also, a crisis effect is clearly visible for Bulgaria, Croatia, Hungary, Romania and Slovenia, which have been dropped in 2008 by a number of their investing partners.

3.2. Network Density

Network density is defined as the fraction of all possible links that are actually present. Table 1 shows definite increases in the network densities of the EEC with the exception of Slovakia (reverting towards pre-crisis levels of connectivity). As sources of investment, Slovenia ranks best, on the 20th position in the database (outranking Austria in terms of number of outward links) followed by Czech Republic (before Malaysia) and Hungary (in between Ireland and Lithuania). As destinations, Poland and Hungary fare best, with rankings similar to Portugal and respectively Cyprus. The laggard networkers are Poland and Romania (as sources of investment) and Slovakia and Latvia (as destinations).

Table 1. Network Density: Outward and Inward Equity Investment. This table reports the outward (i.e. country is a source of investment) and inward (i.e. country is a destination of investment) network density for equity positions of the EEC as well as the total World network density, as well as their rank in the database (within 80 reporting source countries and respectively 241 reported destination countries)

Year	Direction	Country (Rank)											
		Bulgaria	Croatia	Czech Rep.	Estonia	Hungary	Latvia	Lithuania	Poland	Romania	Slovak Rep.	Slovenia	WORLD
2001	Out	0.05 (54/80)		0.13 (39/80)	0.07 (51/80)	0.14 (36/80)			0.16 (32/80)	0.04 (58/80)	0.13 (38/80)		0.09
	In	0.03 (92/241)	0.07 (61/241)	0.10 (49/241)	0.05 (67/241)	0.12 (39/241)	0.03 (93/241)	0.05 (74/241)	0.14 (33/241)	0.08 (56/241)	0.05 (73/241)	0.05 (70/241)	0.09
2002	Out	0.08 (48/80)		0.16 (35/80)	0.10 (45/80)	0.14 (37/80)			0.01 (65/80)	0.04 (57/80)	0.10 (44/80)		0.10
	In	0.02 (109/241)	0.09 (55/241)	0.10 (48/241)	0.08 (56/241)	0.11 (45/241)	0.02 (110/241)	0.04 (83/241)	0.12 (42/241)	0.07 (60/241)	0.04 (80/241)	0.05 (74/241)	0.10
2003	Out	0.06 (55/80)		0.18 (31/80)	0.11 (43/80)	0.16 (36/80)			0.04 (61/80)	0.03 (64/80)	0.10 (47/80)		0.10
	In	0.03 (87/241)	0.10 (51/241)	0.12 (48/241)	0.10 (55/241)	0.12 (45/241)	0.03 (88/241)	0.04 (81/241)	0.13 (41/241)	0.08 (59/241)	0.05 (77/241)	0.05 (67/241)	0.10
2004	Out	0.08 (54/80)		0.20 (29/80)	0.13 (45/80)	0.17 (36/80)			0.05 (60/80)	0.03 (69/80)	0.17 (35/80)		0.11
	In	0.04 (87/241)	0.09 (56/241)	0.12 (48/241)	0.09 (55/241)	0.12 (49/241)	0.04 (88/241)	0.03 (95/241)	0.13 (44/241)	0.08 (64/241)	0.05 (76/241)	0.05 (72/241)	0.11
2005	Out	0.08 (56/80)		0.22 (26/80)	0.18 (39/80)	0.18 (36/80)			0.05 (63/80)	0.05 (64/80)	0.15 (41/80)		0.11
	In	0.07 (74/241)	0.09 (61/241)	0.11 (53/241)	0.09 (60/241)	0.14 (40/241)	0.05 (86/241)	0.06 (80/241)	0.14 (41/241)	0.09 (62/241)	0.05 (85/241)	0.06 (77/241)	0.11
2006	Out	0.12 (50/80)		0.24 (28/80)	0.20 (36/80)	0.24 (29/80)	0.12 (51/80)		0.08 (59/80)	0.05 (65/80)	0.18 (43/80)		0.13
	In	0.09 (72/241)	0.10 (65/241)	0.13 (52/241)	0.08 (73/241)	0.16 (40/241)	0.05 (91/241)	0.07 (82/241)	0.16 (41/241)	0.11 (58/241)	0.05 (90/241)	0.08 (77/241)	0.13
2007	Out	0.12 (54/80)		0.25 (26/80)	0.22 (33/80)	0.20 (38/80)	0.17 (46/80)		0.10 (58/80)	0.06 (65/80)	0.18 (45/80)		0.13
	In	0.11 (60/241)	0.11 (63/241)	0.14 (54/241)	0.10 (65/241)	0.16 (44/241)	0.05 (93/241)	0.08 (77/241)	0.17 (41/241)	0.11 (61/241)	0.05 (98/241)	0.07 (84/241)	0.13
2008	Out	0.15 (48/80)		0.27 (22/80)	0.23 (32/80)	0.27 (23/80)	0.20 (35/80)		0.11 (56/80)	0.07 (61/80)	0.17 (44/80)		0.13
	In	0.09 (70/241)	0.09 (72/241)	0.14 (50/241)	0.09 (65/241)	0.13 (52/241)	0.07 (84/241)	0.09 (71/241)	0.16 (42/241)	0.10 (66/241)	0.06 (93/241)	0.07 (89/241)	0.13
2009	Out	0.20 (39/80)		0.26 (27/80)	0.25 (29/80)	0.26 (28/80)	0.23 (39/80)	0.22 (36/80)	0.08 (66/80)	0.09 (65/80)	0.15 (52/80)	0.34 (20/80)	0.14
	In	0.12 (62/241)	0.10 (65/241)	0.15 (50/241)	0.10 (70/241)	0.15 (48/241)	0.07 (89/241)	0.08 (85/241)	0.17 (43/241)	0.10 (66/241)	0.05 (98/241)	0.10 (67/241)	0.14
2010	Out	0.23 (37/80)		0.31 (25/80)	0.28 (29/80)	0.28 (30/80)	0.24 (35/80)	0.26 (33/80)	0.07 (66/80)	0.09 (62/80)	0.15 (52/80)	0.33 (20/80)	0.15
	In	0.10 (75/241)	0.11 (68/241)	0.15 (55/241)	0.09 (78/241)	0.17 (47/241)	0.06 (95/241)	0.08 (86/241)	0.18 (39/241)	0.12 (62/241)	0.05 (100/241)	0.10 (73/241)	0.15
2011	Out	0.25 (34/80)		0.33 (20/80)	0.20 (42/80)	0.27 (29/80)	0.25 (35/80)	0.25 (33/80)	0.08 (69/80)	0.11 (59/80)	0.14 (55/80)	0.35 (17/80)	0.15
	In	0.10 (69/241)	0.11 (66/241)	0.15 (55/241)	0.10 (72/241)	0.16 (50/241)	0.07 (88/241)	0.08 (85/241)	0.18 (40/241)	0.13 (61/241)	0.05 (102/241)	0.10 (73/241)	0.15
2012	Out	0.25 (31/80)		0.29 (25/80)	0.19 (48/80)	0.28 (28/80)	0.25 (33/80)	0.27 (29/80)	0.10 (64/80)	0.12 (60/80)	0.13 (57/80)	0.33 (20/80)	0.15
	In	0.10 (73/241)	0.11 (68/241)	0.13 (58/241)	0.10 (71/241)	0.18 (44/241)	0.07 (91/241)	0.08 (86/241)	0.20 (35/241)	0.13 (60/241)	0.05 (103/241)	0.10 (74/241)	0.15

The weighted network statistics, where the binary variable (presence/absence of the link) is replaced by the amount invested ($ weight) show that when size of investment is taken into account, only Poland, Czech Republic and Hungary (and to a smaller extent Estonia) stand out in the region and their evolutions mirror closely the global trends including the pre-crisis growth followed by a sharp decline (seen in the Figures 4 as sources and 5 as destinations). The decrease is visibly sharper in $ weights than in number of links, showing that while many links are preserved, the $ exposure is significantly decreased (by exiting relatively important partners country or by reducing positions across many partners). However, post-crisis recovery is visibly slower with the exception of Poland as destination of investment. Of note is also the fact that the EEC are less pro-cyclic as sources of investment and except Croatia, Hungary, Poland and Romania they invest higher amounts abroad than they receive from foreign investors.

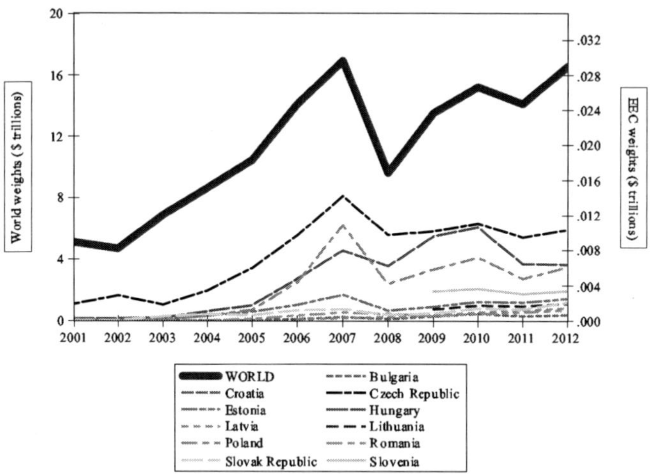

Figure 4. $ Weight of Outward Financial Links. This figure shows the weight in $ trillions of outward financial links (i.e. where the countries represented are seen as sources of investment) of EEC as well as the world total over the period 2001 to 2012.

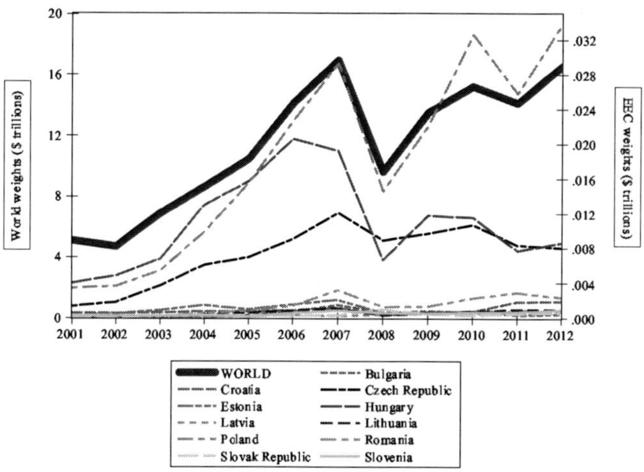

Figure 5. $ Weight of Inward Financial Links. This figure shows the weight in $ trillions of inward financial links (i.e. where the countries represented are seen as destinations of investment) of EEC as well as the world total over the period 2001 to 2012.

3.3. Network Asymmetry

A further tool in describing the network is given by the measures of relative asymmetry measures, expressed in binary (i.e. the presence or absence of a link between two countries) and weighted (i.e. by the $ amount of investment) forms, denoted $AS_{0/1}$ and respectively $AS_{\$}$:

$$AS_{0/1} = \frac{1}{N \times (N-1)} \sum_{i,j \in N} \left| \frac{B(i,j) - B(j,i)}{B(i,j) + B(j,i) + \delta(B(i,j) + B(j,i))} \right|, \quad (1)$$

and

$$AS_{\$} = \frac{1}{N \times (N-1)} \sum_{i,j \in N} \left| \frac{W(i,j) - W(j,i)}{W(i,j) + W(j,i) + \delta(W(i,j) + W(j,i))} \right|, \quad (2)$$

where N is the number of nodes in the network (i.e., economies in the dataset), B and W are the matrices of binary (1/0) and respectively weighted ($ amount) links between the countries and δ is the Dirac delta function. We calculate binary and weighted asymmetry measures for the network consisting of all the 241 economies in our dataset (World) as well as for the subsamples of the EU member states (28 countries) and the EEC (11 countries). Figure 6 shows global asymmetry to be stable (and low, given the large number of countries that - symmetrically - do not connect with each other). Consistent stability seems to be the trademark of the EU network as well in binary terms, while asymmetry in $ terms is overall higher and slightly increasing over the period. Links among the EEC are more dynamic: the binary measure shows visible decrease in 2008 (with Latvia and Poland mutually disconnecting as well as dropping other countries such as Croatia and Romania) that is not in picked up by the $ measure, which shows the sharpest increase. That suggests that the mutual investments of the EEC become increasingly unbalanced. Most recent data points suggest also an incipient tendency of convergence. The increased asymmetry in $ terms during the crisis (2007 - 2008) is due simultaneously to unreciprocated new links (Bulgaria to Poland and Lithuania, Estonia to Croatia and Slovenia), increased holdings (by Czech Republic in Bulgaria, Estonia in Bulgaria, Hungary in Czech Republic, Latvia in Hungary, Slovak Republic in Romania) and decreased holdings (by Czech Republic in Estonia and Hungary, Hungary in Latvia).

While no clear pattern or causality link emerges at this stage (Hungarian stock is at the same more appealing to Latvian investors and less to Czech investors), the question which factors drive international portfolio shifts during the crisis arises.

3.4. Exposure through Counterparties and Clustering

This section identifies the top counterparties of EEC (as sources and destinations of equity investment). A point to be noted is that the maximum amount of reported outward (inward) links for the year 2012 is 78 from Slovenia (48 in Poland) and the minimum number is 25 from Poland (12 in Slovakia). Table 2 lists the Top 20 destinations of equity investments from Eastern Europe in 2012. Financial centres are prominent as receivers (Luxembourg and Ireland being favoured across the board, followed by Switzerland). Germany, France and Russia are also common top destinations followed by Austria, US and UK. Among the Eastern European destinations, Poland, Czech Republic and Hungary attract most of the EEC's equity investments. Table 3 ranks the countries that invest the most in Eastern European economies. Luxembourg and UK are top investors in all the 11 equity markets, followed by US and Sweden. Hun-

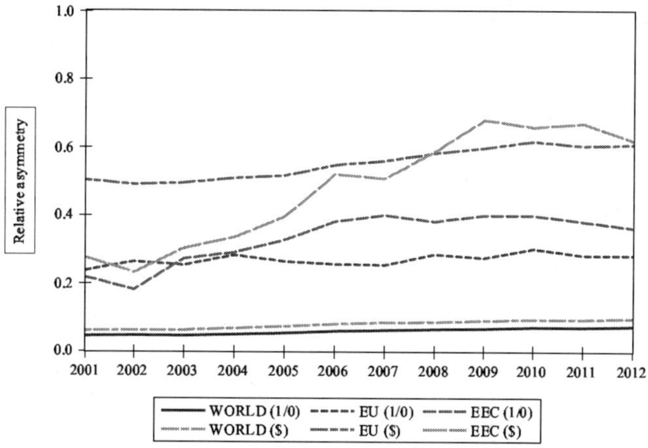

Figure 6. Binary (1/0) and $ Weighted Asymmetry Measures. This figure shows the dynamics of asymmetry measures: binary asymmetry (i.e., presence/absence of link) and weighted asymmetry, (i.e., using $ amounts of investment) for the EEC, the EU as well as the world over the period 2001 to 2012.

gary, Germany, France, Denmark and Austria who are each top investors in 9 of the 11 EEC. Switzerland, Korea and Norway are also well connected, while, among the Eastern European group, Poland, Slovenia and Estonia are the most active (with the same number of East European destinations as Netherlands and Belgium).

Many of the important counterparties of EEC, whose own number of connections is increasing are undoubtedly hubs in the international financial network, thereby channels of increased exposure to worldwide risks. We turn therefore to the evolution of the number of secondary partners (i.e., partners of partners), and respectively a clustering measure CLS, defined as follows:

$$CLS_i = \frac{SL_i}{N_i \times (N_i - 1)}, \tag{3}$$

where SL_i refers to the number of secondary links (i.e., links between partners) of country i and N_i is the number of primary partners of country i.

Table 2. TOP 20: Destinations of Equity Investment of EEC in 2012

TOP	**Bulgaria**	**Czech Rep.**	**Estonia**	**Hungary**	**Latvia**	**Lithuania**	**Poland**	**Romania**	**Slovak Rep.**	**Slovenia**
1	Luxembourg	Luxembourg	Luxembourg	Luxembourg	Luxembourg	Luxembourg	Luxembourg	Austria	US	US
2	US	Belgium	Ireland	US	Ireland	Ireland	Austria	Luxembourg	Germany	Luxembourg
3	France	Austria	Finland	Austria	France	Estonia	Turkey	Poland	Ireland	Austria
4	Ireland	US	France	Poland	Estonia	France	Netherlands	Germany	Luxembourg	Germany
5	Germany	Ireland	US	Germany	Finland	US	Hungary	France	Austria	France
6	Hungary	Jersey	Russia	Ireland	US	Sweden	Russia	Bulgaria	France	Ireland
7	Austria	Germany	Sweden	Czech Rep.	Malta	Finland	France	US	Czech Rep.	UK
8	Czech Rep.	Slovak Rep.	UK	Belgium	UK	UK	Ireland	Canada	Belgium	China
9	Switzerland	France	Latvia	France	Sweden	Russia	Germany	Czech Rep.	UK	Switzerland
10	Russia	UK	Norway	Russia	Russia	Germany	Canada	UK	Russia	Brazil
11	Poland	Russia	Germany	UK	Antigua Barbuda	Austria	Romania	Jersey	Malta	Russia
12	UK	Netherlands	Lithuania	Israel	Belize	Poland	Lithuania	Russia	Poland	Hong Kong
13	Romania	Poland	Turkey	Switzerland	Germany	Latvia	Estonia	Greece	Switzerland	Netherlands
14	Canada	Hungary	Denmark	Turkey	Ukraine	Norway	Slovenia	Cyprus	Japan	Korea
15	Spain	Mauritius	Poland	Slovenia	Lithuania	Romania	Norway	Switzerland	Hungary	Bosnia Herzegovina
16	Turkey	Bermuda	Cayman Islands	Croatia	Cyprus	Bermuda	Korea	Isle of Man	Jersey	Serbia
17	Italy	Switzerland	Switzerland	Jersey	Norway	Malta	Slovak Rep.	Ireland	Korea	India
18	Netherlands	Canada	Czech Rep.	Bulgaria	Austria	Netherlands	Isle of Man	Italy	Netherlands	Croatia
19	Croatia	Malta	Hungary	Netherlands	Canada	Czech Rep.	Spain	Netherlands	Norway	Canada
20	Latvia	Turkey	Ukraine	Canada	Switzerland	Denmark	South Africa	Spain	Turkey	Slovak Rep.

Table 3. TOP 20: Sources of Equity Investment in EEC in 2012

TOP	Bulgaria	Croatia	Czech Rep.	Estonia	Hungary	Latvia	Lithuania	Poland	Romania	Slovak Rep.	Slovenia
1	France	France	US	Luxembourg	US	Norway	Norway	US	US	Czech Rep.	France
2	US	Luxembourg	Luxembourg	Lithuania	Luxembourg	Germany	Germany	Germany	Luxembourg	Jersey	US
3	Greece	US	Jersey	Finland	UK	Jersey	Sweden	UK	Jersey	Belgium	UK
4	Jersey	Austria	UK	US	France	Estonia	Luxembourg	Luxembourg	UK	Slovenia	Korea
5	Romania	Slovenia	Ireland	Sweden	Germany	Luxembourg	Estonia	Jersey	Greece	Korea	Netherlands
6	Cyprus	Germany	Norway	Latvia	Norway	Finland	Poland	Ireland	Sweden	Poland	Luxembourg
7	Hungary	Norway	Germany	Poland	Poland	Sweden	Finland	France	Guernsey	Guernsey	Austria
8	Guernsey	Hungary	Australia	Russia	Ireland	US	UK	Norway	Ireland	UK	Hungary
9	Luxembourg	UK	Hungary	Germany	Netherlands	Lithuania	Latvia	Netherlands	Czech Rep.	Luxembourg	Sweden
10	UK	Guernsey	France	UK	Austria	Hungary	Korea	Guernsey	Gibraltar	Austria	Poland
11	Estonia	Switzerland	Netherlands	France	Czech Rep.	Bulgaria	UK	Hungary	Cyprus	France	Italy
12	Belgium	Sweden	Canada	Italy	Canada	UK	Hungary	Australia	Poland	Bulgaria	Germany
13	Austria	Netherlands	Slovak Rep.	Austria	Australia	Korea	Denmark	Austria	Austria		Estonia
14	Sweden	Estonia	Guernsey	Guernsey	Jersey	Denmark	Russia	Switzerland	Slovenia		Norway
15	Switzerland	Japan	Switzerland	Denmark	Guernsey	Isle of Man	Slovenia	Canada	France		Switzerland
16	Netherlands	Korea	Austria	Slovenia	Switzerland	Mongolia	Switzerland	Sweden	South Africa		Denmark
17	Bahrain	Italy	Sweden	Hungary	Denmark		Iceland	Korea	Germany		Lithuania
18	Denmark	Gibraltar	Japan	Switzerland	Sweden		Brazil	Denmark	Estonia		Romania
19	Slovenia	Lithuania	Denmark	Isle of Man	Korea			Japan	Hungary		Czech Rep.
10	Italy	Denmark	Belgium	Belgium	Bulgaria			Finland	Belgium		Belgium

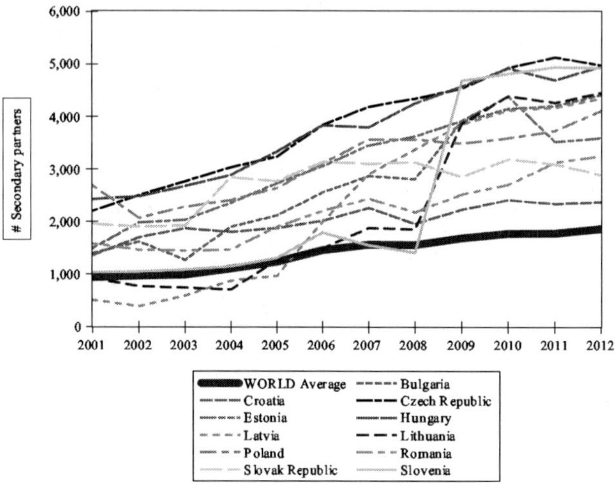

Figure 7. Number of Secondary Partners. This figure shows the number of secondary partners (i.e., partners of primary partners) for EEC as well as the world average over the period 2001 to 2012.

EEC appear more eager to get connected than the average country in the dataset and their increasing number of direct links is translated into the dynamics of their secondary partners. The drop in 2008 is visible for many countries, excepting Czech Republic and the Baltic States (see Figure 7). While the tendency to increase primary and secondary links is common to all the countries, the impact on the clustering measure differs among countries. A maximum clustering measure of 1 implies that all the primary links of a country form links among themselves. A country with few selected connections is therefore more apt to be part of a cluster. Figure 8 shows that most EEC start in this situation, but their dynamics differ over the period. Compared to the world average clustering which is remarkably stable (and high due to a high number of countries with extremely low connections), EEC are clearly divided into two groups: on one side Croatia, Poland, Romania and Slovak Republic in closer than average clusters while the remaining countries (Bulgaria, the Baltic States, Hungary and the Czech Republic) are exploring more open networks. While on average increasing the number of partners leads to more open networks, at times the reverse might be true, if the new partners are connected to the existing partners or if the dropped partners were connected to other direct partners.

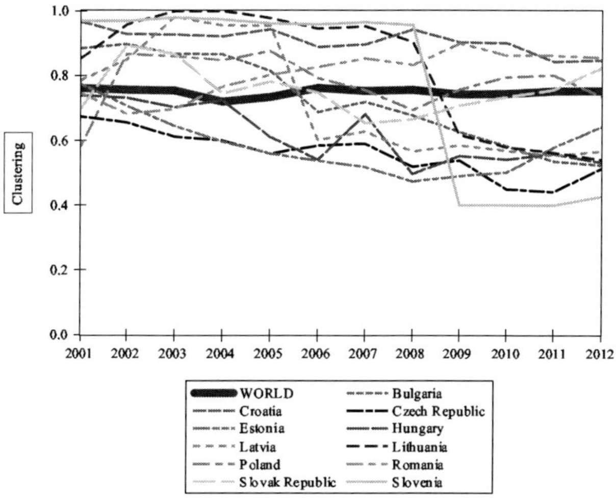

Figure 8. A Measure of Clustering. This figure shows the dynamics of a measure of clustering, i.e., the proportion of existing links between pairs of partners in the number of links possible, for EEC as well as the world average over the period 2001 to 2012.

3.5. Correlations and Centrality

There is a positive correlation between the number of links of each country and the $ amount of investment that goes through those links. A higher number of links channel more money, but when the correlations increase, it suggests that the changes to the network involve partners with higher than average $ weight and when the correlations decrease it suggests that the changes involve partners with lower than average $ weight.

Figure 9 shows the dynamics of correlations between the number of inward and outward financial links and their $ weight for the complete dataset, as well as the EU and EEC subsamples. While correlations are strongly positive (with a higher number of partners linked with larger equity values), the differences in patterns are relevant. World correlations are perfectly stable for destinations, but slowly decreasing for sources suggesting that the higher number of receiving partners have lower $ weight. A visible reversal occurs over 2008, which corroborated with the drop in connections documented earlier suggests that connections of significant $ weights have been dropped. For the EU, the correlations

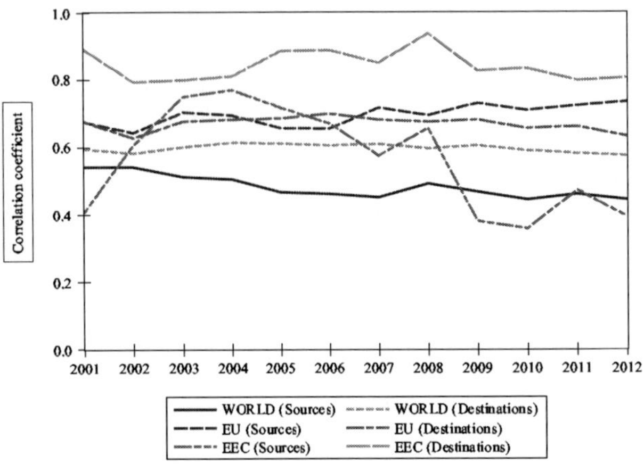

Figure 9. Correlation between Number of Financial Links and Weights ($). The number of financial links and their weights for the EEC, the EU as well as the world over the period 2001 to 2012.

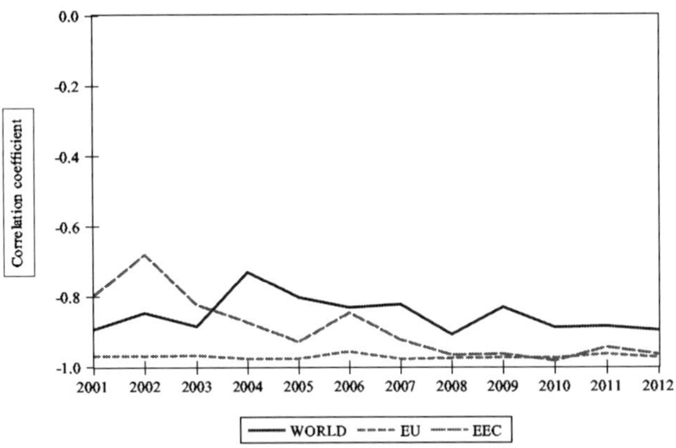

Figure 10. Correlation between Number of Partners and Clustering. This figure shows the dynamics of correlation coefficients between the number of partners of a country and the clustering measure for the EEC, the EU as well as the world over the period 2001 to 2012.

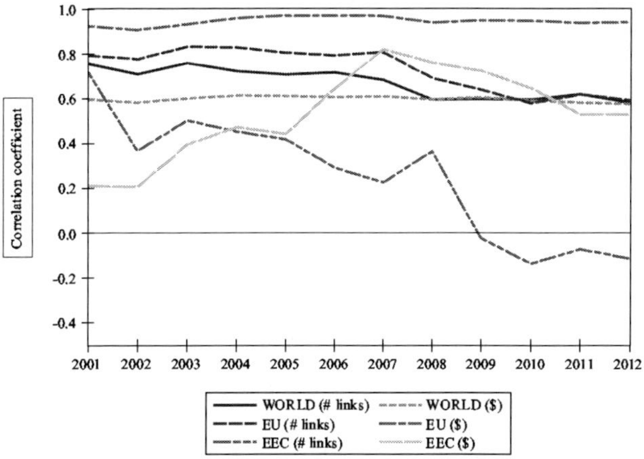

Figure 11. Correlation Between Sources and Destinations. This figure shows the dynamics of correlation coefficients between sources and destinations (number of links and respectively $ weights) for the EEC, the EU as well as the world over the period 2001 to 2012.

are higher than in the wider dataset, suggesting the newer links have similar $ exposure. A slight divergence towards the end of the period (between the increasing source correlations and the decreasing destination correlations) suggest that EU countries themselves choose destinations of higher $ weight but as destinations they receive lower $ amounts. There appears to be no discernible crisis effect in the EU. The EEC experience a crisis effect both as sources and as destinations, with increasing correlations in 2008, suggesting that they reduced their exposures to significant partners and in turn, they have been discarded by some of their partners. On the whole, when the EEC are sources of investments, the correlations between the number of receiving countries and $ amounts invested are relatively low (and decreasing), which suggests that the new partners of EEC have relatively low $ weight. Slovenia provides a good example of this strategy (as can be seen in Section 4).

Figure 10 gives further insight. There is a strong negative correlation between number of partners and the clustering measure (i.e., the proportion of partners that are also trading with each other), showing that increasing the number of partners decreases clustering. For the EU, the correlations are almost perfectly stable and at the extremity of the negative range, which suggests that newly formed or newly dropped links involve partners out of the "clan". A crisis effect points to this becoming also the case worldwide (though the pattern is considerably less smooth). Post 2008, EEC's strategy is aligned with that of the EU as a whole.

Figure 11 shows a positive relationship between the number of inward and outward links at world and European level typically stable in $ terms, but decreasing in terms of the number of links. The correlation in $ terms of inward and outward amounts is highest for EU showing that their dynamics are almost perfectly in sync. A post-crisis decline in the inward and outward links correlations suggest that partnerships have been reviewed (and the dynamics of in and out partners are increasingly divergent) possibly with the aim of maintaining a balance between $ amounts. The patterns are similar but more dramatic for the heterogeneous sample of East European countries, where the correlation between the number of inward and outward links drops below 0 towards the end of the sample, when notably Slovenia, a small, outward looking country with many destinations but comparably fewer sources, starts to report its holdings of foreign equity assets. The EEC range goes from Slovenia to Poland the largest country in the region which distributes its holdings among fewer partners, while at the same time attracting the largest number of foreign equity investors.

4. Country Focus

This section zooms in to investigate the individual choices of foreign partners of the EEC in an exploratory exercise. We identify the significant partners of our countries of interest and look for patterns in their investment strategies, especially the period of the financial crisis (2007-2008). Significant destinations are defined as countries that have at any time during the sample period accounted for more than 5% of the annual foreign assets of a EEC and respectively, significant sources are countries that hold at any time during the sample more than 5% of the foreign liabilities of a EEC. United States, Austria, France, Germany are significant partners common to most EEC. A recurrent pattern is also the heavy investment via financial centers (apart from Luxembourg, the other significant ones are Ireland, Bermuda, British Virgin Islands, Cayman Islands) which obscures the final destinations and leaves open the possibility that the EEC are more diversified than it would appear. Despite the veil of these indirect investments, an informative representation of the EEC's choices of partners is still possible.

4.1. Bulgaria

Bulgaria appears heavily biased towards investing in Luxembourg and US as destinations (even increasingly so with the former reaching 75% in 2012 and the latter 86% in 2011). Its main significant partners are Austria, France, Germany, US (same as the rest of its neighbours) but also Italy and Finland. Notably, Russia (a fellow Slavic country) holds 17% of the Bulgarian foreign equity assets (in 2007) and Greece (its Southern neighbour) holds 10% in 2008. The only EEC of note for Bulgaria are Romania (the Northern neighbour) and Hungary.

As a destination country, Bulgaria offers more visibility and more diversification (with a larger number of significant sources - 16 - and lower portfolio weights). While part of Bulgarian stock is sold via Luxembourg (a significant partner in every year) as well as other financial centres, the top investor is clearly the neighbouring Greece followed by the US. In fact, the interest is mutual since during the financial crisis, when Bulgaria virtually exits the US market, Greece is the main beneficiary. As expected, there are significant investments from other developed European markets such as Austria, Germany, France, UK and Italy. Among the EEC as investors, neighbouring Romania ranks 4th in 2011 with 6% and Estonia (following Denmark, Sweden and Finland) had significant interests in Bulgarian equity before the crisis.

4.2. Croatia

Croatia does not report its foreign holdings and is covered by our dataset only as a destination of investment. As such, it has 15 significant investors over the period. Austria (a country with strong historical ties) accounts for over 70% of the Croatian foreign liabilities in 2011 and 2012 displacing US and Germany at the top. Luxembourg is the ever present channel of investment, followed by Ireland and other financial centres, but UK, France and Italy together with Norway and Sweden make themselves present in their own name. The ex-Yugoslav neighbour, Slovenia as well as Hungary and Estonia are partners of note among the EEC.

4.3. Czech Republic

Czech Republic also acquires about 40% of its foreign equity holdings through a financial centre, switching over the period from Cayman Islands to Luxembourg. Belgium and the Netherlands are added to the list of common destinations among the developed markets. Slovak Republic (the former twin) is the only EEC partner of note and also benefits from a strong counter-cyclical increase in investment in 2008.

Czech Republic as a destination is less revealing, with only 9 significant investors, 4 of which being financial centres. However, the unchallenged top investor in Czech equity is US, holding every year 30-40% of Czech foreign liabilities. UK, Belgium, Denmark and the neighbouring Poland are the declared followers.

4.4. Estonia

Estonia's portfolio appears significantly more balanced, avoiding the extreme concentration of other EEC. The top two destinations always add up to less than 50% of the total foreign assets, which by the region's standards is a performance. When Luxembourg is in the first place, Finland (with over 20% of holdings in 2002), a maritime neighbour and Poland (over 10% in 2005) are next in significance. Another element that supports the view that Estonia is actively more diversified is the fact that no less than 16 countries achieve significance over the period and many among them are EEC: Latvia, Hungary, Lithuania, Croatia, Poland and Romania. During the crisis, Estonia decreases its position in Finland only in 2008, and quickly recovers it in 2009.

Apart from the typical developed markets that are common destinations to all EEC, Estonia's particular partners are Sweden (a relatively close Scandinavian country) and Russia (the significant Eastern neighbour).

Estonia's top investments in equity come via Luxembourg as well as from Scandinavian countries (Finland, Sweden) or the other Baltic States (Latvia and Lithuania) holding about 10-20% of Estonian foreign equity liabilities. US fades in significance over the years while Poland is repeatedly a top investor.

4.5. Hungary

Hungary's top destination choice, Luxembourg, replaces US and absorbs 20-40% of the country's portfolio. Relevantly, the third place is disputed among Austria (neighbour of strong historical links), Poland and Germany. In 2006 and 2007, Austria manages to outrank US. Other developed markets (France, UK, but also Netherlands) are significant on more than one occasion together with Russia and among the EEC, Czech Republic.

Hungary's top investor is the US, with a steadily declining share, just below 30% in the last three years, followed always by Luxembourg. UK and France are common investors followed by Austria, Netherlands and Norway. Slovak Republic made a significant investment only in 2003.

4.6. Latvia

About half of Latvia's portfolio is veiled by investment in Luxembourg (always first and increasing its weight up to over 40%) and Ireland (about 10% in many years). The typical developed destinations (France, US) are complemented with an expected regional flavour by Scandinavian countries (Finland, Norway and Sweden), neighbouring Russia and Estonia. In crisis, Estonian equity gains more weight in the Latvian foreign equity holdings.

Norway, Germany, Sweden, Finland and Denmark have all followed the US as the top investors in Latvia. In 2011 and 2012, Norway and Germany held together 80% of Latvian foreign liabilities. Estonia is the only other declared investor while financial centers account for less than 10% of the foreign held Latvian shares.

4.7. Lithuania

Lithuania follows suit, with even more of its assets (about 50% to 60%) going through Luxembourg and Ireland. France, Austria and US are followed by the expected Northerners: Finland, Estonia and Sweden (the latter being the most significant of the country's neighbours).

As a destination, Lithuania is a mirror of its neighbour Latvia with Norway and Germany holding as much as 70% of the portfolio together. Sweden, Finland, Denmark as well as Luxembourg are the only other major players in recent years. Estonia is above our 5% threshold of significance up to 2008.

4.8. Poland

Poland comes from a completely undiversified position (holding in 2001 a staggering 97% of its foreign assets in US stock) and its channel of diversification is Luxembourg (absorbing a third of its portfolio in all other years). Austria, Netherlands and Turkey vie for the following positions with significant holdings below 20%. During the crisis Poland decreases its holdings in all these countries and opens a position in German stock (10%). France is significant only in early years and notably Hungary is a constant presence since 2003.

Poland's top investor is the US (30%) followed at some distance by neighbouring Germany and UK (about 10%) as well as undisclosed investors via Luxembourg and other financial centres. France and Norway are the only countries whose contributions are significant in a large market such as Poland.

4.9. Romania

Romania's portfolio only chance of diversification lies behind its equity investments in Luxembourg, which is in most years one of the top destinations. The Top 2 partners account for more than 70% of Romanian foreign assets in 9 years. Austria represents 85% of the foreign equity assets held by Romania in 2006 and together with Luxembourg absorbs up to 90% and 75% of the Romanian foreign equity investment in 2007 and respectively 2008. By comparison, all other destinations are secondary. They tend to be Germany, Italy, France, UK and the Netherlands and notably and recurrently Moldova (a neighbour of common historical roots). In crisis (2007-2008), Romania increased dramatically and temporarily its positions in German stock. Since 2009, the neighbour whose position is steadily growing is Bulgaria.

Romanian equity's top buyers have been typically based in US, Netherlands, Greece and Sweden. UK as well as Austria and Estonia (before the crisis) were also recurring investors, while financial centers channel up to 20% of Romanian foreign held equity.

4.10. Slovak Republic

Slovak Republic's portfolio has a history of being heavily unbalanced (at the beginning of the sample), Hungary weighing more than 60% two years in a row (2003 and 2004) after Czech Republic and Germany held the lion share in the previous years (30% and respectively 40%). United States is the top destination in 2012 with over 20% of foreign assets (having switched places with Luxembourg in previous years). The common developed markets (Austria, France, Germany) are complemented by Belgium, Netherlands and on occasion Cyprus. While Hungary becomes an insignificant partner, Czech Republic is understandably a constantly important presence. Moreover, in 2008, its weight in the Slovak portfolio doubled.

There is no prize for naming Slovak Republic's top investor, with a portfolio weight of at least 40% every year since 2002. Czech Republic comes second only on three occasions: to Luxembourg in 2001, to Austria in 2003 and to Italy in 2009. US, Belgium, Poland and Slovenia are the only other names of reference.

4.11. Slovenia

Slovenia presents an interesting pattern. While it is the country with most outward links, these many destinations receive relatively insignificant amounts and Slovenia's only significant partners are US, Austria, France, Germany and Luxembourg. Excesses have been avoided (in contrast with some of the other EEC). Its prominent destination is US (20% to 25% of total foreign equity assets held by Slovenians) with Austria, Germany and Luxembourg following with about 10%. France never fails to end the Top 5. Although only 4 years of data are available, Slovenia appears not to reshuffle its portfolio and weights are remarkably stable. Among its neighbours, it favours Austria.

Neighbouring Italy was the traditional top investor in Slovenia (with portfolio weights as high as 60-70% in the early years, till 2004), challenged in more recent years (successfully on occasion) by US and France (the top positions holding about 30% of Slovenian foreign held equity). UK, Austria, Germany and Sweden are persistent with Hungary and Czech Republic making only occasionally the significance threshold.

5. Conclusion and Budding Hypotheses

While the current exercise is neither concerned with judging optimality of investment strategies nor with examining strictly defined hypotheses through statistical testing, it has the more flexible objective of letting the Eastern European foreign equity investment data "speak freely" in order to uncover patterns and hypotheses for future testing. The first part of the chapter is concerned with positioning the EEC in the international financial network, where they appear to be increasingly connected nodes, either outward looking (Slovenia) or attractive to a large number of foreign investors (Poland). The second part reflects upon the EEC's choice of partners in equity investments, where group behaviour is apparent, especially through the existence of micro-groups or pairs of geographically and historically close neighbours. A reader of the Section 4 focusing on the investment strategies of individual countries would hardly err in the task of linking a given description of the choice of partners to the country of origin. Zooming in even closer, we note that each country tends to favour one of its neighbours as a destination and the following pairs of rising (sometimes counter-cyclically) neighbourly investment are uncovered: Bulgaria - Greece, Czech Republic - Slovak Republic, Estonia - Finland, Hungary - Austria, Latvia - Estonia, Lithuania - Sweden, Poland - Germany, Romania - Bulgaria (displacing Moldova), Slovak Republic - Czech Republic, Slovenia - Austria.

We are zooming out of the region with further research questions to be generalized and tested empirically. It has been established that the international financial network is a dynamic entity that expands and contracts over time and that suffered the impact of the financial crisis of 2007-2009. This chapter illustrated the dynamic (as yet unsettled) behaviour of the EEC within the network. Their position appears to gaining in importance overall which increases their exposure to global risks and the need to analyze their strategic choices. In this vein, the significant neighbourly preferences of each of the EEC raise questions regarding the interplay of financial reasoning versus cultural factors in international portfolio choices especially under the stress of the global crisis.

References

Allen, F. and A. Babus (2009). *Networks in Finance*, Chapter 21, pp. 367–382. Pearson Education.

Allen, F. and D. Gale (2000). Financial contagion. *The Journal of Political Economy* 108, 1–33.

Babus, A. (2007). The formation of financial networks. Tinbergen Institute Disscussion Paper 06-093.

Battiston, S., D. Delli Gatti, M. Gallegati, B. Greenwald, and J. Stiglitz (2012). Liaisons dangereuses: Increasing connectivity, risk sharing and systemic risk. *Journal of Economic Dynamics and Control* 36, 1121–1141.

Chinazzi, M., G. Fagiolo, J. Reyes, and S. Schiavo (2012). Post-mortem examination of the international financial network. *Working Paper*.

In: Non-Linear Modeling … ISBN: 978-1-63484-932-6
Editors: L. Liviu Albu and P. Caraiani

Chapter 4

IMPACT OF MONETARY POLICY ON STOCK MARKET IN CEE COUNTRIES

Corina Sâman[*]
Institute for Economic Forecasting,
Romanian Academy, Bucharest, Romania

ABSTRACT

This chapter analyze the impact of monetary policy on three Central European stock markets (the Czech Republic, Hungary, Poland) and Romania. The transmission of monetary policy through the influence of short-term interest rates on asset prices (including longer-term interest rates and stock prices) is important because it determines private borrowing costs and changes in wealth, which influence real economic activity. These relationships are important to monetary policymakers which are interested in estimations of the reactions of asset prices to monetary policy and also to financial market participants which need to make reliable investment decisions and formulate appropriate risk management strategies.

Most of the studies typically relate stock returns to measures of monetary policy in the context of single equation specifications and/or multivariate Vector Autoregressions (VAR's). In this chapter we focus on the nonlinearity of the short-run relation. We find a negative and significant relation between 1-month interest rate, as a proxy for

[*] Casa Academiei, 13 Septembrie no. 13, Institute for Economic Forecasting, Bucharest, Romania. Email: csaman@ipe.ro.

monetary policy, and stock markets returns for Romania and partially in a second regime for all other three CEE countries.

Keywords: monetary policy, CEE stock market, TAR model, CEE countries, Romania
JEL Classification: E44, E47, E52

INTRODUCTION

The impact of monetary policy on the economy could be measured by the changes it determines in macroeconomic variables like output, employment or inflation, but this effect can be observed with delay.

The response of stock prices returns to exogenous monetary policy is mostly direct and immediate so it could give an insight in the efficiency of the monetary policy on the real economy. The relationship is important to monetary policymakers who are interested in estimations of the impact to monetary policy and also to financial market participants which need to make reliable investment decisions and formulate appropriate risk management strategies.

In recent years, reflecting the importance of this issue, a growing number of empirical studies have documented the negative relationship between monetary policy and the stock market.

Home and Jaffrey (1971) shows that money supply had a significant linear effect on stock price. Jensen and Johnson (1995) also find that monetary policy developments are associated with patterns in stock returns. They found that the impact of discount rate on stock returns is asymmetric higher and less volatile on decreases than those of discount rate increases.

Thorbecke (1997) used orthogonalized innovations in monthly federal funds rate and non-borrowed reserves to capture the effects of monetary shocks on industry level returns over the period 1967 to 1990. He shows that monetary policy shocks have a large positive effect on monthly stock returns that is more pronounced for smaller capitalization stocks.

Conover, Jensen and Johnson (1999) shows that not only US stock returns, but also returns on foreign markets are related with US monetary environments (as well as their local monetary environment). The study of Lastrapes (1998) found that monetary policy had an impact on stock price. Rigobon and Sack (2002) analysed the effect of monetary policy measured by federal funds interest rate on stock returns and discovered that an increase in short-term interest rates results in a decline in stock prices.

Ehrmann M. and Fratzscher M. (2005) found that individual stocks reacted heterogeneously to U.S. monetary policy shocks. They showed that firms with more financial constraints are affected significantly more by monetary policy.

Bjornland H. C. and Leitemo K. (2009) found great interdependence between the interest rate setting and real stock prices. Kholodilin K. et al. (2009) showed that the ECB's monetary policy had a heterogeneous impact on the sectoral stock market indexes in the Euro Area.

Other studies like Bohl M.T. et al. (2008), Basistha and Kurov (2008), Jansen and Tsai (2010) and Syed Mujahid Hussain (2011) investigated the response of Major European and/or US equity indices to unexpected interest rate decisions by central banks. Bohl M.T. et al. (2008) studied the reaction of European stock market returns to surprising interest rate decisions by the European Central Bank (ECB) and found evidence of a negative and significant effect. Syed Mujahid Hussain (2011) found that the effect of monetary policy surprises on both the returns and volatility of stock prices is in the majority of cases contemporaneous and significant. Basistha and Kurov (2008), Jansen and Tsai (2010) studied the asymmetric relationship between the monetary policy and stock returns and found the response of stock returns to monetary surprises in a bear market is large, negative, and statistically significant.

Also, Hsu, K-C and Chiang, H-C (2011) employing smooth transition autoregressive (*STAR*) models investigate the nonlinear effect of monetary policy (expressed by the change in the federal fund rate) on excess returns of stock prices and found out that the impact is larger in a bear-market regime than in a usual regime.

In this chapter we study monetary policy in relation to the stock price focusing on the nonlinearity of the short-run relation. We do not intend to analyse the reaction of CEE stock market returns to unexpected interest rate decisions of central banks so we do not apply an event-study methodology (Kuttner 2001, Thorbecke 1997), or an analysis based on *VAR* models (Peersman 2002, Christiano et al. 1999), or the identification through heteroskedasticity approach of Rigobon and Sack (2004). Instead we choose to estimate the nonlinear relationship among monetary policy, net stock returns, and output growth by using the *TAR* model.

We choose to estimate *TAR* models instead of *STAR* because we want to test the hypothesis of differential effects of money market interest rate on stock returns across two market regimes.

DATA

This chapter uses monthly data from March 2000 to June 2015 (184 observations). We use monthly percentage change in the stock index in local currency (hereafter *NR*) as stock prices; the first difference of the 1-month market interest rate as proxy variable of the monetary rate (hereafter *Dir*) and the growth rate of industrial production (hereafter *Gip*). This specific period is chosen due to data availability and to the fact that it contains the last financial crisis beginning in 2008, which supports the idea that the relationship should be nonlinear. All data are collected from EUROSTAT and DATASTREAM databases. Figure 1 shows the time series plot of stock index net return, *Dir*, and *Gip* for Romania. Figure 2 shows the same plot for Poland.

The stock price indexes considered are BET for Romania, BUX for Hungary, Prague SE PX for the Czech Republic and POLWIGI for Poland.

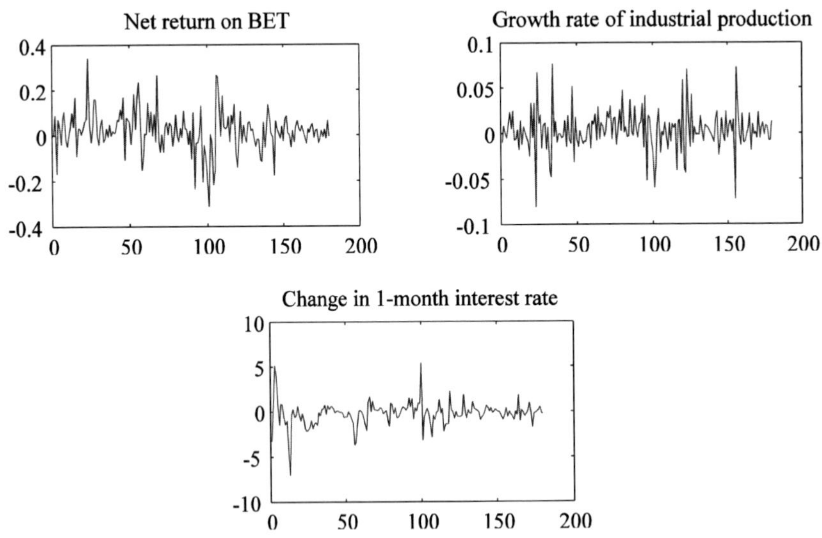

Figure 1. Net Return, Change in 1-month interest rate, and growth rate of industrial production for Romania. July 2000 to June 2015.

METHODOLOGIES AND EMPIRICAL RESULTS

In the presence of nonlinearities, the linear conventional methodologies determine inefficient estimations and inference tests with low power. One solution to deal with nonlinear data generation process is the threshold models introduced by Balke and Fomby (1997), and further developed by Enders and Granger (1998), Enders and Siklos (2001), Hansen and Seo (2002).

The two-regime threshold model is an estimation procedure that formulates a two-regime threshold autoregressive TAR model:

$$x_t = \theta_1' X_{t-1} I_{\{Z_{t-d}<\lambda\}} + \theta_2' X_{t-1} I_{\{Z_{t-d}\geq\lambda\}} + e_t \text{ , } t = 1 \dots T \qquad (1)$$

where x_t is a p-dimensional I(1) time series for $t = 1,2,...,T$, $X_{t-1} = (1, x_{t-1}, \dots, x_{t-l})'$, $I_{\{\bullet\}}$ is the Heaviside indicator function, e_t is an i.i.d. disturbance, the transition variable Z_{t-d} where d is the delay parameter that will be determined endogenously. The threshold value λ is also unknown and takes the values in the compact interval $\lambda \in \Lambda = [\lambda_1, \lambda_2]$, where λ_1 and λ_2 are selected according to $P(Z_t \leq \lambda_1) = \pi_0$ and $P(Z_t \leq \lambda_2) = 1 - \pi_0$. In this paper we use $\pi_0 = 0.15$. [1]

Equation (1) indicates that the model follow regime 1 when the threshold exceeds or is equal to the threshold value; otherwise it follows regime 2. If there is no significant difference between the estimated parameters, i.e., $\theta_1 = \theta_2$, the threshold model collapses into a linear model as in equation (1). The model allows us to estimate the regime-dependent parameters and the threshold value (λ) endogenously.

The proposed estimation procedure is maximum likelihood under the assumption that the errors are i.i.d. Gaussian. For a threshold error-correction model with p=2 a grid search over the two-dimensional space (β, λ) was chosen by Hansen and Seo as a suitable algorithm for the maximization that is no smooth.

The test for the presence of threshold is SupLM test (proposed by Davies, 1987) whose asymptotic distribution depends on the covariance of the data

[1] For π_0 between 0.05 and 0.15 this division provides the optimal trade-off between various relevant factors, which include the power of the test and the ability of the test to detect the presence of a threshold effect (Andrews, 1994).

(Hansen and Seo, 2002). The null hypothesis (there is no threshold, the model is linear) is tested against the hypothesis of two-regime threshold model (1).

$$SupLM = \sup_{\lambda\in\Lambda=[\lambda_1,\lambda_2]} LM(,\lambda) \qquad (2)$$

[2]

Building Threshold Models

The first step in estimating a threshold model is to estimate a linear autoregressive model based on informational criteria.

The second step is to search over possible transition variables and over the possible value for the delay d. The identification procedure should be based on the test for the appropriateness of *TAR* model, *SupLM*. The threshold value λ is determined by a grid search with 300 grid points and p_values calculated by parametric residual bootstrap computed with 5000 simulation replications as in Hansen and Seo (2002) is used to assess the evidence for threshold model.

The final step is to estimate the threshold model. The validity of the models with two regimes is asserted by the p-value of the Test for Equality of Dynamic Coefficients.

The Granger Causality Tests examine whether all the coefficients of Δx_{1t-i} are jointly statistical different from zero.

The Empirical Model and Results

All three variables can be considered endogenously determined following a *TAR* model.

The equation for net return (NR) can be written as:

$$\begin{aligned} NR_t &= (a^1 + \sum_{i=1}^{k11} \delta_{1i}{}^1 NR_{1t-i} + \sum_{i=0}^{k12} \delta_{2i}{}^1 Dir_{1t-i} + \sum_{i=0}^{k13} \delta_{3i}{}^1 Gip_{1t-i}) I_{\{Z_t<\lambda\}} \\ &+ (a^2 + \sum_{i=1}^{k11} \delta_{1i}{}^2 NR_{1t-i} + \sum_{i=0}^{k12} \delta_{2i}{}^2 Dir_{1t-i} + \sum_{i=0}^{k13} \delta_{3i}{}^2 Gip_{1t-i}) I_{\{Z_t\geq\lambda\}} + e_t \end{aligned} \qquad (3)$$

---

[2] Also for maximization a grid search over the interval for λ is performed in Hansen and Seo (2002).

The equation for the difference in interest rate:

$$\begin{aligned} Dir_t &= (b^1 + \sum_{i=1}^{k21} \gamma_{1i}{}^1 NR_{1t-i} + \sum_{i=1}^{k22} \gamma_{2i}{}^1 Dir_{1t-i} + \sum_{i=1}^{k33} \gamma_{3i}{}^1 Gip_{1t-i}) I_{\{Z_t<\lambda\}} \\ &+ (b^2 + \sum_{i=1}^{k21} \gamma_{1i}{}^2 NR_{1t-i} + \sum_{i=1}^{k22} \gamma_{2i}{}^2 Dir_{1t-i} + \sum_{i=1}^{k33} \gamma_{3i}{}^2 Gip_{1t-i}) I_{\{Z_t\geq\lambda\}} + e_t \end{aligned} \tag{4}$$

And for the growth rate in industrial production:

$$\begin{aligned} Gip_t &= (b^1 + \sum_{i=1}^{k31} \varphi_{1i}{}^1 NR_{1t-i} + \sum_{i=1}^{k32} \varphi_{2i}{}^1 Dir_{1t-i} + \sum_{i=1}^{k33} \varphi_{3i}{}^1 Gip_{1t-i}) I_{\{Z_t<\lambda\}} \\ &+ (b^2 + \sum_{i=1}^{k31} \varphi_{1i}{}^2 NR_{1t-i} + \sum_{i=1}^{k32} \varphi_{2i}{}^2 Dir_{1t-i} + \sum_{i=1}^{k33} \gamma_{3i}{}^2 Gip_{1t-i}) I_{\{Z_t\geq\lambda\}} + e_t \end{aligned} \tag{5}$$

The transition variable can be one of any of the three variables, different for each equation. The decision about the proper lag length of the transition variable *d* (can be any number from 1 to 3 inclusive) is made based on the test for the appropriateness of *TAR* model, *SupLM*. The hypothesis of linearity is rejected at 5%-10% significance level corresponds to the highest statistics.

The results for *NR* equation are presented in tables 1-4 for Romania and respectively for the Czech Republic, Hungary and Poland. Table 3 shows that for Hungary the transition variable is *NR* and the delay is 3. For all other countries the interest rate differential is selected based on the rejection of linearity hypothesis with 5% level of significance for Romania and 10% level for the Czech Republic, and Poland.

Table 1. The SupLM test for *NR* equation – The case of Romania

Transition variable	NR_{t-d}	Dir_{t-d}	Gip_{t-d}
d = 0		8.1493 (0.3734)	81.9368 (0.0028)*
d = 1*	14.4385 (0.1094)	17.3611 (0.0144) *	14.4384 (0.1206)
d = 2	10.5176 (0.338)	8.0904 (0.664)	10.5176 (0.348)
d = 3	11.7944 (0.2288)	12.8876 (0.0974)	11.7944 (0.2254)

Note: p-values are in (). * indicates the selected variable and the lag length.

Table 2. The SupLM test for *NR* equation – The case of the Czech Republic

Transition variable	NR_{t-d}	Dir_{t-d}	Gip_{t-d}
d = 0		9.9322 (0.1446)	9.2092 (0.4482)
d = 1*	11.5929 (0.0831)	9.4554 (0.1696)	9.3023 (0.4422)
d = 2	9.4701 (0.6116)	11.8100 (0.0728) *	11.4011 (0.1876)
d = 3	9.4040 (0.515)	8.8649 (0.2292)	

Note: p-values are in (). * indicates the selected variable and the lag length.

Table 3. The SupLM test for *NR* equation – The case of Hungary

Transition variable	NR_{t-d}	Dir_{t-d}	Gip_{t-d}
d = 0		8.6574 (0.1712)	
d = 1*	5.9263 (0.2898)	4.3060 (0.6134)	8.0511 (0.2197)
d = 2	6.8971 (0.1896)	8.0752 (0.2024)	5.9393 (0.4108)
d = 3	9.1875 (0.0788) *	8.8175 (0.1634)	7.8742 (0.221)

Note: p-values are in (). * indicates the selected variable and the lag length.

Table 4. The SupLM test for *NR* equation – The case of Poland

Transition variable	NR_{t-d}	Dir_{t-d}	Gip_{t-d}
d = 0		13.0834 (0.089)	11.4826 (0.3164)
d = 1*	10.8614 (0.4116)	13.5324 (0.0688) *	8.7598 (0.7068)
d = 2	11.5573 (0.1782)	11.0390 (0.1836)	10.5320 (0.475)
d = 3	12.6764 (0.1998)	9.3657 (0.3042)	8.6924 (0.7316)

Note: p-values are in (). * indicates the selected variable and the lag length.

The results of model estimates of Eq. (3) are shown in Tables 5-8. The second column in reports the estimates of the linear *AR* model and the third and fourth column shows the coefficients of the *TAR* model for the two regimes.

The linear models for CEE countries indicate a positive effect of the changes in the interest rate on stock returns. This is unusual so the question is if the linear models presents the real situation or not and if a separation in two regimes better reflect the influence of monetary policy on stock return.

The results from the test of linearity and the informational criteria (Akaike and Bayesian) show that the linear models are performing worth than a two-regime autoregressive (TAR).

The validity of the models with two regimes is asserted by the p-value of the test for Equality of Dynamic Coefficients that is less than 5% for all countries with the exception of Poland.

The results for Romania indicate that the change in the 1-month interest rate has a negative and statistically significant effect on stock net returns. It indicate that a contractionary monetary policy reduces stock returns as demonstrated by the findings of most of the literature. The majority of observations (77.78%) locates in the high excess regime where the first difference of the monthly interest rate Dir $_{t-1}$ is larger than the estimated threshold value -0.81.

Table 5. The models of net returns on stock prices - The case of Romania

Model/ variable	Linear	TAR - Threshold Estimate (Dir $_{t-1}$) -0.81	
		First Regime 22.22% observations	Second Regime 77.78% obs.
constant	0.007785 (0.007200)	0.060331 (0.021408)	0.008788 *0.007015)
NR $_{t-1}$	0.063172 (0.082425)	0.212452 (0.115952)	-0.041977 (0.105862)
Dir $_t$	-0.011665 (0.008026)	-0.016761 (0.005872)	-0.005097 (0.011541)
Dir $_{t-1}$	-0.016727 0.008331	0.013982 (0.009939)	-0.026524 (0.014650)
Gip $_{t-2}$	0.537055 0.270990	0.819565 (0.589967)	0.511390 (0.299676)
Gip $_{t-3}$	0.536451 0.293432	1.562463 (0.518532)	0.253792 (0.334037)
		Wald Test for Equality of Dynamic Coefficients	
		12.968515 p_value= 0.0237	
AIC	-4.846406	-4.951666	
BIC	-4.829388	-4.934648	

Note: Numbers in parenthesis are Eicker-White standard errors or p-values for the tests.

In the usual net returns regime, the coefficient of *Dir* is -0.005097 - 0.026524 = -0.03162, which indicate that monetary policy has larger effects on stock returns than in the first regime (the coefficient is -0.00278 = -0.016761 + 0.013982). In other words, monetary policy has larger effects on stock returns when it is contractionary.

The coefficients of Gip_{t-2} and Gip_{t-3} are weaker in the usual returns regime when $Dir_{t-1} > -0.81$.

This shows that when the monetary policy is not so tight an increase in the growth rate of industrial production can significantly increase the net returns.

For the other three CEE countries, the effect of monetary policy (the change in the 1-month interest rate) has not a clear negative and statistically significant effect on stock net returns. For the Czech Republic, the monetary policy is effective in majority of observations (84.44%) that belongs to the second regime.

The coefficients of Gip_{t-2} and Gip_{t-3} are weaker in the usual returns regime when $Dir_{t-2} > -0.14$. This shows that when $Dir_{t-1} < -0.14$ (a decrease in interest rate) an increase in the growth rate of industrial production can increase more the stock returns than when the change in interest rate is positive or has a low negative value.

Table 6. The models of net returns on stock prices - The case of the Czech Republic

Model/ variable	Linear	TAR - Threshold Estimate(Dir_{t-2}) -0.14	
		First Regime 15.56% observations	Second Regime 84.44% obs.
constant	0.002350 (0.005452)	0.024231 (0.012456)	0.000541 (0.005755)
NR_{t-1}	0.103005 (0.096616)	-0.268184 (0.247516)	0.151989 (0.085482)
Dir_t	0.000405 (0.052807)	0.270293 (0.108763)	-0.081351 (0.034529)
Gip_{t-2}	0.317564 (0.274356)	0.844688 (0.611679)	0.159705 (0.301404)
Gip_{t-3}	0.513881 (0.322420)	1.099447 (0.817548)	0.517941 (0.326832)
		Wald Test for Equality of Dynamic Coefficients	
		16.5899 p_value=0.0023	
AIC	-5.350598	-5.491763	
BIC	-5.333580	-5.474745	

Note: Numbers in parenthesis are Eicker-White standard errors or p-values for the tests.

For Hungary and Poland, in the usual net returns regime, the coefficient of Dir_t is positive and significant in more than 70% of cases. This issue must be further investigated using event-study approach or incorporating into the study other sources besides tight money that might increase the riskiness of stocks and so reducing the stock returns. It can be noticed in figure 2 that the fluctuation on *Dir* variable in the first four years is larger than the rest of the sample period.

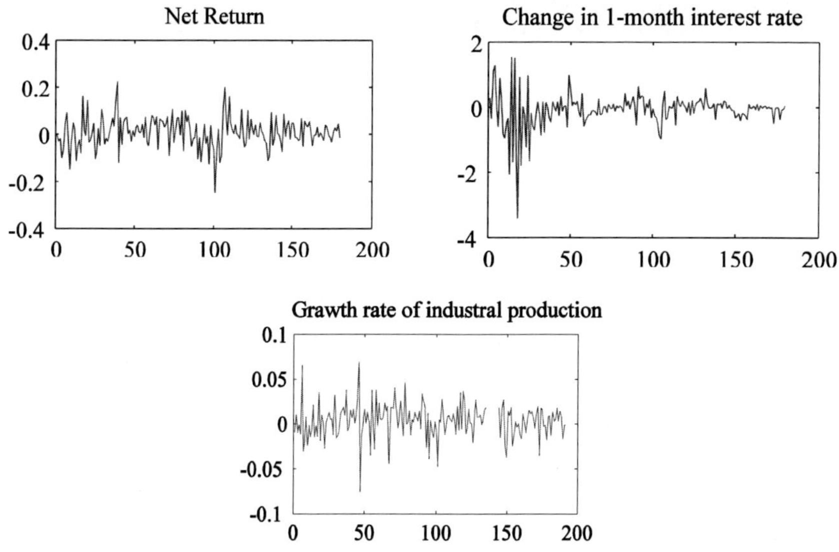

Figure 2. Net Return, Change in 1-month interest rate, and growth rate of industrial production for Poland. July 2000 to June 2015.

Table 7. The models of net returns on stock prices - the case of Hungary

Model/ variable	Linear	TAR - Threshold Estimate(NR_{t-3}) 0.0531	
		First Regime 76.11% observations	Second Regime 23.89% obs.
constant	0.004377 (0.005229)	0.001581 (0.005730)	0.019283 (0.010396)
NR_{t-1}	0.104651 (0.085967)	0.065064 (0.097226)	0.242200 (0.175380)
Dir_t	-0.018774 (0.010789)	0.003333 (0.007821)	-0.048776 (0.016269)
Gip	0.415420 (0.202340)	0.408812 (0.209607)	0.500018 (0.429367)
Wald Test for Dir Granger Cause NR (p_value)		0.669948	0.002717
		Wald Test for Equality of Dynamic Coefficients	
		11.618784 p_value= 0.0088	
AIC	-5.256761	-5.332182	
BIC	-5.239743	-5.315164	

Note: Numbers in parenthesis are Eicker-White standard errors or p-values for the tests.

For Poland, the threshold value of the transition variable is positive (0.11) suggesting that a more constraint monetary policy is needed in order to have the expected negative effect on stock returns.

Table 8. The models of net returns on stock prices - the case of Poland

Model/ variable	Linear	TAR - Threshold Estimate(Dir_{t-1}) 0.11	
		First Regime 73.33% observations	Second Regime 26.67% obs.
constant	0.003720 (0.004790)	0.012028 (0.006120)	-0.007915 (0.011435)
NR_{t-1}	0.076218 (0.090437)	0.141346 (0.091992)	-0.093627 (0.159961)
Dir_t	0.005284 (0.010569)	0.019465 (0.010986)	-0.033762 (0.021339)
Gip_{t-2}	-0.001992 (0.009039)	0.008994 (0.010731)	-0.009415 (0.022685)
Gip_{t-3}	0.664219 (0.266596)	0.599309 (0.292133)	0.831987 (0.438880)
		Wald Test for Equality of Dynamic Coefficients:	
		8.729965 p_value = 0.120332	
		Wald Test for *Dir* Granger Cause *NR*:	
		3.601288 (0.1652)	3.273552 (0.1946)
AIC	-5.387176	-5.476287	
BIC	-5.370158	-5.459269	

Note: Numbers in parenthesis are Eicker-White standard errors or p-values for the tests.

The result of the Granger test for causality shows that it could not be rejected the hypothesis that change in interest rate doesn't cause growth rate in stock prices.

CONCLUSION

For some of the Central and Eastern European (CEE) countries, the linear models indicate a positive effect of the changes in the interest rate on stock returns. This is unusual so the question is if the linear models presents the real situation or not and if a separation in two regimes better reflect the influence of monetary policy on stock return. To find a response to this question a two regime autoregressive (*TAR*) model is employed.

The evidence concerning the significance of the response of stock returns to the monetary policies is proved to be inconclusive for the Czech Republic, Hungary and Poland. The results presented in this chapter show that an increase in the 1-month interest rate has a negative effect on net returns in the case of high contractionary monetary policy regime when decreases stock returns for all three CEE countries. In the case of a lighter policy the effect is not always negative as expected. As suggested by Hsu, K-C. and H-C. Chiang (2011) financial constraints could be one cause of inconclusive results.

This issue must be further investigated following a different approach, like event-study or by incorporating into the analysis more assets as suggested in Bernanke and Kuttner (2005) or other sources besides tight money that might increase the riskiness of stocks.

For Romania, the contractionary monetary policy has a negative effect on net returns regardless of the magnitude of the increase in the interest rate.

ACKNOWLEDGMENTS

The work was supported by a grant of the Ministry of National Education CNCS – UEFISCDI project number PN-II-ID-PCE-2012-4-0631.

REFERENCES

Andrews, D. 1993. “Tests for parameter instability and structural change with unknown change point.” *Econometrica 61*: 821–856.

Basistha, A., and A. Kurov. 2008. “Macroeconomic cycles and the stock market’s reaction to monetary policy.” *Journal of Banking and Finance* 32:2606–2616.

Bernanke, Ben S. and Kenneth N. Kuttner. 2005. “What Explains the Stock Market’s Reaction to Federal Reserve Policy?” *The Journal of Finance* 60(3):1221-1257.

Bohl, M. T., Siklos, P. L., and Sondermann, D., 2008. “European Stock Markets and the ECB’s monetary Policy Surprises. “*International Finance* 11(2):117-130.”

Chen, S. S. 2007. ”Does monetary policy have asymmetric effects on stock returns?” *Journal of Money, Credit, and Banking* 39:667–688.

Christiano, Lawrence J., Martin Eichenbaum and Charles Evans. 1999. “The Effects of Monetary Policy Shocks: Evidence from the Flow of Funds.” *Review of Economics and Statistics* 78(1), 16-34.

Conover, M., Jensen, G., and R. Johnson. 1999. “Monetary Environments and International Stock Returns.” *Journal of Banking and Finance* 23:1357-1381

Davies, R. B., 1987. “Hypothesis testing when a nuisance parameter is present only under the alternative.” *Biometrica* 74: 33-43.

Ehrmann, M., and M. Fratzscher. 2004. "Taking Stock: Monetary Policy Transmission to Equity Markets." *European Central Bank Working paper Series*, no. 354.

Gali, J. and L. Gambetti. 2013. "The Effects of Monetary Policy on Stock Market Bubbles: Some Evidence. " Available at: <*www.wiwi.uni-frankfurt.de/kolloquium/ss14/Gali.pdf*>.

Hansen, B. E., and B. Seo. 2002. "Testing for two-regime threshold cointegration in vector error-correction models." *Journal of Econometrics* 110: 293-318.

Jensen, G., and R. Johnson. 1995. "Discount Rate Changes and Security Returns in the US, 1962-1991." *Journal of Banking and Finance* 19:79-95.

Kholodilin, K., et al. 2009. "Assessing the Impact of the ECB's Monetary Policy on the Stock Markets: a Sectoral View." *Economics Letters* 105(3):211-213.

Kuttner, Kenneth N. 2001. "Monetary Policy Surprises and Interest Rates: Evidence from the Fed Funds Future Market." *Journal of Monetary Economics* 47(3), 523-544.

Hsu, K-C. and H-C. Chiang. 2011. "Nonlinear effects of monetary policy on stock returns in a smooth transition autoregressive model." *The Quarterly Review of Economics and Finance* 51(4):339-349.

Jansen, W. D., and C.-L. Tsai. 2010. Monetary policy and stock returns: Financing constraints and asymmetries in bull and bear markets." *Journal of Empirical Finance* 17:981–990.

Lastrapes, W. D., 1998. "International Evidence on Equity Prices, Interest Rates and Money." *Journal of International Money and Finance* 17(3):377-406.

Michael, E. and Marcel, F., 2005. "Equal Size, Equal Role? Interest Rate Interdependence Between the Euro Area and the United States." *Economic Journal*,115(506):928-948.

Peersman, Gert. 2002. "Monetary Policy and Long Term Interest Rates in Germany." Economics Letters 77(2), 271-277.

Rigobon, R. and B. P. Sack. 2004. "The Impact of Monetary Policy on Asset Prices." *Journal of Monetary Economics* 51(8):1553-1575.

Syed, M. H., 2011. "Simultaneous Monetary Policy Announcements and International Stock Markets Response: an Intraday Analysis." *Journal of Banking and Finance*, 35(3):752-764.

Thorbecke, W., 1997. "On Stock Market Returns and Monetary Policy." *Journal of Finance* 52(2):635-654.

In: Non-Linear Modeling … ISBN: 978-1-63484-932-6
Editors: L. Liviu Albu and P. Caraiani

Chapter 5

A REAL-TIME DAILY COINCIDENT INDICATOR FOR ROMANIAN ECONOMY

Marius Acatrinei [*]
Institute for Economic Forecasting, Bucharest, Romania

ABSTRACT

We construct a real-time daily coincident indicator for Romanian economy by extracting information from an unbalanced panel of daily, monthly and quarterly data with the help of the Harvey accumulator. We use a mixture of financial and macroeconomic data. By using a dynamic factor model transposed in a state-space framework, we can extract the daily unobserved common component. The indicator is a measure of the Romanian business conditions. In the second part we apply a Bayesian Markov-Switching with three states to the indicator for inferring the turning points in the business conditions and measure the duration of the recessions. Since the results showed that the indicator may provide significant real time information about the state of the economy and about the disequilibria latently accumulating in the economy well before the official release of the GDP, the indicator may be used as an early warning indicator for economic distress for Romanian economy.

[*] Marius Acatrinei, PhD. Email: marius.acatrinei@gmail.com.

Keywords: business cycle, dynamic factor model, nowcasting, state space model, turning points, recession, Markov-Switching

INTRODUCTION

A daily business indicator can be an important tool for policy makers since it combines information stemming from a variety of sources, both macroeconomic and financial dataset, and thus provides a clear signal of the current direction of the business conditions with few months in advance of the official data releases. Such an indicator can make the most of information on the correlation structure of the macroeconomic and financial data by yielding a single indicator easy to interpret and understand.

Furthermore, since a real-time indicator of the business conditions should inform on the latest changes in macroeconomic data, it should make use of intra-monthly and monthly data in order to auto-update at each new release.

Evans (2005) seminal paper opened a new chapter in the real-time estimation of GDP at high frequencies, by modelling the dynamics of GDP similarly to business conditions. He used state-space models to estimate a daily GDP growth from monthly and quarterly data. One of the drawbacks of the model is that it can handle only a limited number of time series.

Since using a large number of time series is problematic in the standard VAR models, dynamic factor models (DFM) are the preferred choice among macroeconomists for nowcasting GDP. The DFM considers that a limited number of unobservable factors, called dynamic factors, drive the dynamics of the GDP or of the business conditions. Kalman filter is one of the methods used to extract the dynamic factors once DFM is represented in a state space model. Maximum likelihood estimation uses Kalman filtering to estimate the state space formulation of the DFM. Forni, Hallin, Lippi and Reichlin (2000), Stock and Watson (2002a, 2002b, 2003), Boivin and Ng (2006) had important contributions in this area of research among others.

Burns and Mitchell (1946) considered that any business cycle has two main characteristics: a) co-movement between economic variables through the economic cycle and b) a regime switching at the turning points of the business cycle. Hamilton's paper (1989) models nonlinearity in the business cycle and separates two phases of the business cycle by using a Markov Switching model. Hamilton (2011) reviews the most important methodologies used for dating business cycle turning points and predicting recessions.

The non-synchronicity of macroeconomic data releases poses a problem when modelling large and unbalanced datasets. In order to incorporate all the information from unbalanced datasets, Giannone, Reichlin and Small (2008) had used a dynamic factor model.

Their model uses a large number of time series (200 time series) which are released at different times and with different lags. By doing so, the authors can evaluate the impact of each release on the GDP nowcast and also to interpret the data releases in comparison with the model filtered data for each time series. The model summarizes the information from the time series with a few common factors. Then the GDP forecast is defined as "the projection of quarterly GDP on the common factors estimated from the panel of monthly data." In the first estimation step, the principal components are extracted from a balanced panel by exploiting the collinearity of the series, while in the second step the common factors are extracted using the Kalman smoother on the unbalanced dataset.

Banbura and Modugno (2014) have shown how to link the filtered estimates for each variable with the nowcast revision. The authors imposed restrictions on the principal components loadings for reflecting the temporal aggregation.

A "coincident index of economic activity" is closely related in terms of methodology to the GDP nowcasts since they are both estimated with dynamic factor models with a state space representation. A state space model has two equations: a) "measurement equation" which links the observed time series with the unobservable factors and b) the "transition equation" which defines the law of motion for the state vector (unobservable factors) which may have variables with higher frequencies.

Stock and Watson (1988) proposed a single-index linear dynamic factor model in order to analyze the co-movements between industrial production, employment, income and sales by assuming that a single factor could capture the dynamics of the business cycle. The Conference Board publishes the Composite Index of Coincident Economic Indicators (CEI). Other coincident indicators are published by Aruoba, Diebold and Scotti (ADS, 2009), the Chicago Fed National Activity Index (CFNAI), the Eurocoin index produced by Bank of Italy and the Euro-STING model of Camacho and Perez Quiros (2010).

Camacho and Perez-Quiros (2010) estimated a coincident indicator for European business cycle using a single factor model (Stock and Watson, 1988). The model handles the "ragged ends" as proposed by Giannone, Reichlin and Small (2008), mixes monthly and quarterly frequencies as in

Mariano and Murasawa (2003) and deals with data revisions for GDP growth as in Evans (2005) which assumes that the flash releases are equal to the true GDP plus uncorrelated noise.

Anderson and Gascon (2009) used state space models to estimate GDP for the US economy using all available data sets, including data revisions.

Albu (2008) was the first researcher who estimated a composite index of economic activity for Romanian economy using monthly data.

Aruoba, Diebold and Scotti (2009) estimated an index of economic activity (x_t) based on four observable indicators sampled daily, weekly, monthly and quarterly. For the first time in the nowcasting literature the authors included data with daily frequency, while other models used only monthly and quarterly data.

The originality of the Aruoba, Diebold and Scotti (2009) may be summarized by four main ideas:

1. Since the Business cycle is the interplay of several macroeconomic variables, the economic theory suggests that the business conditions are a latent factor. The authors assume that the indicator has an autoregressive structure of order 1 (AR1) and evolves daily. The daily unobservable indicator for the business conditions is denoted x_t.

$$x_t = \rho x_{t-1} + e_t, \textit{where } e_t \textit{ is white noise} \tag{1}$$

2. Since information about the business conditions show up at different frequencies, it is important to incorporate the information as it comes in order to update the indicator;

3. Since high frequency indicators such bond yield or equity returns may supply critical information about financial market expectations, it is important to incorporate them;

4. Since mixed frequency models may lead to complications due to the temporal aggregation of stock and flow data, the extraction of the latent indicator is carried out linearly with the Kalman filter.

Following their research, the Philadelphia FED publishes weekly a daily coincident index extracted from the following dataset: daily term spread, weekly initial jobless claims, monthly payroll employment, industrial production, personal income less transfer payments, manufacturing and trade sales and quarterly real GDP[1].

[1] The model's results for the United States are available at http://www. philadelphiafed.org/ research-and-data/real-time-center.

The following analysis is motivated by the Aruoba, Diebold and Scotti (2009) paper. We have estimated in the first part of the chapter a daily coincident indicator for Romanian business conditions by applying a dynamic factor model to a dataset with different frequencies. We used daily, monthly and quarterly data between Q3 2007 – Q3 2015 in order to extract a daily unobservable factor for the Romanian business conditions.

In the second part, following Kim, Nelson and Starz (1998) we have fitted a Markov Switching model with three in order to infer the transition probabilities of the indicator. Brave and Butters (2010) applied a similar model to the index of Aruoba, Diebold and Scotti (2009).

The advantages of the proposed approach is that it may identify fast and in real-time changes in the business cycle. … While in United States the NBER Committee officially identifies and date stamps the business cycle phases, there are not official data for the Romanian business cycle. In this respect we consider that this chapter may provide a fresh outlook on the measurement of the business conditions for Romanian economy.

DATA

We noted the time series with superscript for each frequency such as y_t^i $(i = 1, \cdots 4)$. We used the following time series:

1) y_t^1 is the daily term premium calculated as the difference between 10 year TBill and 6 month debt certificate issued by the Finance Minister. The data are stationary since they are differences of yields. The data are measured daily and are stock variables. There are no gaps in the dataset[2];
2) $\tilde{y}^3_{\text{indprod}}$ is the industrial production index; flow variable. The data are monthly, published by the National Institute of Statistics with a 2 month lag[3]. The data are volume and constant price value index and are seasonally adjusted;
3) $\tilde{y}^3_{\text{roesi}}$ is the Economic Sentiment Indicator (ESI). The data for Romanian ESI are published at the end of the month with 1 month

[2] The data are available on Thomson Reuters Datastream.

[3] The data are available on http://www.insse.ro/cms/en/content/industrial-production-index.

lag[4];flow variable. The data are published by DG ECFIN as part of a business survey;

4) $\tilde{y}^3_{\mathrm{employment}}$ are monthly employment data and include, according to the methodology of "Household labor force survey" all persons aged 15 years and over. The date are a stock variable, volume not seasonally adjusted. We have deseasonalized the data with Demetra+ Tramoseat procedure;

5) y^4_{gdp} are quarter-on –quarter growth of real GDP between Q2 2007 – Q2 2015. The GDP data are chain linked volumes (2010) at market prices, seasonally adjusted and adjusted data by working days[5]. The GDP data are flow data.

The employment data, industrial production and Economic Sentiment Indicator for Romania were detrended with the Hodrick Prescott filter which removes the smoothed trend from the seasonally adjusted series and extracts the cyclical component. The GDP data were stationarized by taking logarithm differences. We performed Philips-Perron tests to test for unit root on the transformed data.

STATE SPACE MODEL WITH DAILY DATA

The "observed" business cycle indicators $y_t^i \ (i = 1, \cdots 4)$ at a daily frequency are specified as follows:

$$y_t^i = \beta_i x_t + \gamma_i y_{t-D_i}^i + u_t^i \qquad (2)$$

where $\mathrm{D_i}$ is the number of days from the observation period (ex: $\mathrm{D_i} = 7$ for weekly data)

Broadly speaking, the low frequency data are considered high frequency data with missing observations. This is the reason why there are needed the aggregators defined below. The aggregators link the observed low frequency data with the unobserved high frequency component.

---

[4] The data are available on http://ec.europa.eu/economy_finance/db_indicators/surveys/time_series/index_en.htm.

[5] The data are available on Eurostat.

The low frequency indicators evolve daily although they are observed only at lower frequencies. Therefore $\tilde{y}_t^i$ represent the high frequency but unobservable data (y_t^i) at a lower frequency (tilde frequency).

The relationship between $\tilde{y}_t^i$ and y_t^i is functionally bounded on the type of data. The stock variable represents variables measurable at a particular point in time, while flow variable are measured with reference to a period of time.

Stock Variables:

$$\begin{cases} \tilde{y}_t^i = y_t^i = \beta_i x_t + \gamma_i y_{t-D_i}^i + u_t^i, \text{if } y_t^i \text{ is observed} \\ \tilde{y}_t^i = NA \end{cases} \tag{3}$$

If a stock variable is measured at a lower frequency, then at any time the value of the observed stock variable is identical with the tilde value, namely $\tilde{y}_t^i = y_t^i$. If the stock variable is not observed, then we record NA as missing observations. The stock variables depend on the daily coincident index and their own lagged values.

On the other hand, a flow variable observed at a lower frequency ($\tilde{y}_t^i$) is measured as a sum of daily values.

Flow Variables:

$$\begin{cases} \tilde{y}_t^i = \sum_{j=0}^{D_i-1} y_{t-j}^1 \text{ if } y_t^i \text{ is observed} \\ \tilde{y}_t^i = NA \end{cases} \tag{4}$$

If a flow variable is measured at a lower frequency, then at any time the value of the observed flow variable is a sum of y_{t-j}^i if the data are observed on day t and is NA otherwise.

Taking into account that the flow variables depend also on exogenous variables and serially uncorrelated innovations, the equation for the flow variables may be written as:

$$\tilde{y}_t^i = \beta_i \sum_{j=0}^{D_i-1} x_{t-j}^i + \gamma_i \sum_{j=0}^{D_i-1} y_{t-D_i-j}^i + \sum_{j=0}^{D_i-1} u_{t-j}^i \tag{5}$$

Given that $\tilde{y}_t^i = \sum_{j=0}^{D_i-1} y_{t-j}^i$ and $\sum_{j=0}^{D_i-1} u_{t-j}^i = u_t^{*i}, Var(u_t^{*i}) = D_i * Var(u_t^i)$ then the equation may be written as

$$\tilde{y}_t^i = \beta_i C_t^{D_i} + \gamma_i \tilde{y}_{t-D_i}^i + u_t^{*i} \quad (6)$$

where accumulator variable $C_t^{D_i}$ adds up the daily flows over all days in the observational period (e.g., week) and is defined as follows:

$$C_t^{D_i} = \xi_t^{D_i} C_{t-1}^{D_i} + x_t \quad (7)$$

where $\xi_t^{D_i} = 0$ if t is the first day of the observational period and $\xi_t^{D_i} = 1$ otherwise.

In this chapter we apply the ADS's implementation of the Harvey (1990) accumulator for monthly and quarterly sums. The accumulator is useful in managing the missing data. By using the accumulator it is possible to expand the state vector α_t with a deterministically evolving indicator that is a summary of all past values of the unobserved factor aggregated such as to correspond with the low frequency of the observed data.

The stock variables do not need an aggregator of the past realization. On the other hand flow variables that correspond to sums or averages over the higher base frequency of the factor do need an aggregator that accumulate the factor realizations over a defined period in order to account for the contemporaneous factors' contribution to the observed data.

The accumulator for sum variables is denoted by $C_t^{D_i}$ (ex: weekly, monthly, and quarterly). The sum accumulator represents the sum of all of the factor realizations that happened within the current period of the lower frequency of observation (e.g., a week).

The accumulator is defined recursively and it is included in the state vector. The daily shocks u_{t-j}^i of the flow variable are summed over the observation period for obtaining the shocks at a lower frequency (tilde frequency) u_t^{*i}.

Measurement equations

$$y_t = Z\alpha_t + \Gamma w_t + \varepsilon_t, \varepsilon_t \sim (0, H_t) \quad (8)$$

$$\tilde{y}_t^1 = \beta_1 X_t + u_t^1$$
$$\tilde{y}_{indprod,t}^3 = \beta_2 C_{indprod,t}^m + \gamma_1 \tilde{y}_{indprod,t-m}^3 + u_{1,t}^{*3}$$
$$\tilde{y}_{roesi,t}^3 = \beta_3 C_{roesi,t}^m + \gamma_2 \tilde{y}_{roesi,t-m}^3 + u_{2,t}^{*3}$$

$$\tilde{y}^3_{employment,t} = \beta_4 x_t + \gamma_3 \tilde{y}^3_{employment,t-m} + u^3_t$$
$$\tilde{y}^4_{gdp,t} = \beta_5 C^q_t + y_4 \tilde{y}^4_{gdp,t-q} + u^{*4}_t \tag{9}$$

$$\begin{bmatrix} y^1_t \\ \tilde{y}^3_{indprod,t} \\ \tilde{y}^3_{roesi,t} \\ \tilde{y}^3_{employment,t} \\ y^4_{gdp,t} \end{bmatrix} = \begin{bmatrix} \beta_1 & 0 & 0 & 0 & 1 \\ 0 & \beta_2 & 0 & 0 & 0 \\ 0 & 0 & \beta_3 & 0 & 0 \\ \beta_4 & 0 & 0 & 0 & 0 \\ 0 & 0 & 0 & \beta_5 & 0 \end{bmatrix} \begin{bmatrix} x_t \\ C^m_{indprod,t} \\ C^m_{roesi,t} \\ C^q_{gdp,t} \\ u^1_t \end{bmatrix} +$$

$$\begin{bmatrix} 0 & 0 & 0 & 0 \\ \gamma_2 & 0 & 0 & 0 \\ 0 & \gamma_3 & 0 & 0 \\ 0 & 0 & \gamma_4 & 0 \\ 0 & 0 & 0 & \gamma_5 \end{bmatrix} \begin{bmatrix} \tilde{y}^3_{indprod,t-m} \\ \tilde{y}^3_{roesi,t-m} \\ \tilde{y}^3_{employment,t-m} \\ \tilde{y}^4_{gdp,t-q} \end{bmatrix} + \begin{bmatrix} 0 \\ u^{*3}_{1,t} \\ u^{*3}_{2,t} \\ u^3_{3,t} \\ u^{*4}_{4,t} \end{bmatrix},$$

$$H = \begin{bmatrix} 0 & 0 & 0 & 0 & 0 \\ 0 & \sigma^{*2}_{2,t} & 0 & 0 & 0 \\ 0 & 0 & \sigma^{*2}_{3,t} & 0 & 0 \\ 0 & 0 & 0 & \sigma^2_{4,t} & 0 \\ 0 & 0 & 0 & 0 & \sigma^{*2}_{5,t} \end{bmatrix} \tag{10}$$

The vector of observed variables is denoted y_t and includes the following variables: the daily term premium, industrial production index, Economic Sentiment Indicator for Romanian economy, employment and real GDP growth (q-o-q). The y_t dataset contain many missing observations due to the fact that the variables are observed at lower frequencies, with the exception of daily term premium. The main idea is to treat all variables *as if* they are all observed at a daily frequency.

The vector w_t containes lagged dependent variables for all variables with the exception of daily term premium.

The state vector α_t includes the following state (unobservable) variables:

- x_t is the coincident daily index for business conditions;
- C^m_t is the monthly accumulator. Since we have two monthly (flow) variables, we have two accumulators: $C^m_{indprod}$ for the Industrial Production Index and C^m_{roesi} for the Romanian ESI (European Sentiment Indicator);
- C^Q_t is the quarterly accumulator for the (real) GDP data;

- u_t^1 are the innovations for the daily coincident index which is an AR (1) error process for the daily yield curve premium. The daily yield curve premium is the empirical "slope" of the yield term structure. The errors for the other variable are not written in the state vector since they are related with their unobserved values and are summed over the whole time (monthly, quarterly).

The vector w_t includes the following state variables:

- $\tilde{y}^3_{indprod,t-m}$ is 1 month lagged industrial production ($\tilde{y}^2_{t-m}$ or $\tilde{y}^2_{t-30}$);
- $\tilde{y}^3_{roesi,t-m}$ is 1 month lagged European Sentiment Indicator for Romanian economy;
- $\tilde{y}^3_{employment,t-m}$ are 1 month lagged employment data;
- $\tilde{y}^4_{gdp,t-q}$ is 1 quarter lagged real GDP ($\tilde{y}^4_{t-m}$ or $\tilde{y}^4_{t-90}$).

Transition equations

$$\alpha_{t+1} = T\alpha_t + R\eta_t, \eta_t \sim (0, Q) \tag{11}$$

$$\begin{aligned} x_{t+1} &= \rho x_t + e_t \\ C^m_{indprod,t+1} &= \rho x_t + \xi^m_{1,t+1} C^m_{indprod,t} \\ C^m_{roesi,t+1} &= \rho x_t + \xi^m_{2,t+1} C^m_{roesi,t} \\ C^q_{gdp,t+1} &= \rho x_t + \xi^q_{3,t+1} C^q_{gdp,t} \\ u^1_{t+1} &= \gamma_1 u^1_t + \zeta_t \end{aligned} \tag{12}$$

$$\begin{bmatrix} x_{t+1} \\ C^m_{indprod,t+1} \\ C^m_{roesi,t+1} \\ C^q_{gdp,t+1} \\ u^1_{t+1} \end{bmatrix} = \begin{bmatrix} \rho & 0 & 0 & 0 & 0 \\ \rho & \xi^m_{1,t+1} & 0 & 0 & 0 \\ \rho & 0 & \xi^m_{2,t+1} & 0 & 0 \\ \rho & 0 & 0 & \xi^q_{3,t+1} & 0 \\ 0 & 0 & 0 & 0 & \gamma_1 \end{bmatrix} \begin{bmatrix} x_t \\ C^m_{indprod,t} \\ C^m_{roesi,t} \\ C^q_{gdp,t} \\ u^1_t \end{bmatrix} + \begin{bmatrix} 1 & 0 \\ 0 & 0 \\ 0 & 0 \\ 0 & 0 \\ 0 & 1 \end{bmatrix} \begin{bmatrix} e_t \\ \zeta_t \end{bmatrix}, Q = \begin{bmatrix} 1 & 0 \\ 0 & \sigma^2_{1t} \end{bmatrix} \tag{13}$$

where

ξ^w_{t+1} is 1 when the monthly values are accumulating, 0 otherwise;
ξ^q_{t+1} is 1 when the quarterly values are accumulating, 0 otherwise.

The first state equation allows for the possibility that the first state variable has a unit root.

In order to extract the state vector and obtain smoothed estimates of the signal (y_t), we estimate the model with the Kalman Filter. We present very briefly the Kalman filter.

Kalman Filter

$$\alpha_{t|t} = \alpha_t + P_t Z_t' F_t^{-1} \upsilon_t \tag{14}$$

$$P_{t|t} = P_t - P_t Z_t' F_t^{-1} Z_t P_t' \tag{15}$$

$$\alpha_{t+1} = T\alpha_{t|t} \tag{16}$$

$$P_{t+1} = TP_{t|t}T' + RQR' \tag{17}$$

where

$$\upsilon_t = y_t - Z_t\alpha_t - \Gamma_t w_t$$
$$F_t = Z_t P_t Z_t' + H_t$$
$$\alpha_{t|t} \equiv E(\alpha_t|Y_t)$$
$$P_{t|t} = var(\alpha_t|Y_t)$$
$$\alpha_t \equiv E(\alpha_t|Y_{t-1})$$
$$P_t = var(\alpha_t|Y_{t-1})$$
$$Y_t = \{y_1, \dots y_t\}$$

In the second step, we fit a Bayesian Markov-Switching model with three states (Kim, Nelson and Starz, 1998) for the coincident indicator extracted above. We difference and demean the indicator and we test for stationarity with Philips-Perron test.

$$x_t \sim N(0, \sigma_t^2) \tag{18}$$

$$\sigma_t^2 = \sigma_1^2 S_{1t} + \sigma_2^2 S_{2t} + \sigma_3^2 S_{3t} \tag{19}$$

$$S_{kt} = 1 \text{ if } S_t = k \text{ and } S_{kt} = 0, k = 1,2,3 \tag{20}$$

$$P[S_t = j|S_{t-1} = i] = p_{ij} \text{where } i, j = 1,2,3 \quad (21)$$

$$\sum_{j=1}^{3} p_{ij} = 1 \quad (22)$$

where x_t is the differenced coincident indicator for business conditions and S_t is the unobservable variable that follows a first-order Markov chain with transition probabilities. We have used noninformative priors and estimated the state variable (S_t) with a multimove Gibbs sampler (Kim and Nelson, 1998).

RESULTS

The extraction of the state vector was carried out with the Kalman smoother. A more detailed explanation of the Kalman filter can be found in Durbin and Koopman's book (2012).

Table 1. Parameters values

Nr.crt	Variable	Coeff	Std.Error	T-Stat	Signif
1.	β_1	0.0535	0.1843	0.290	0.77
2.	β_2	0.0159	0.0050	3.130	0.00
3.	β_3	0.0116	0.0033	3.534	0.00
4.	β_4	0.1471	0.0340	4.322	0.00
5.	β_5	0.0142	0.0042	3.385	0.00
6.	γ_1	0.9871	0.0028	340.5	0.00
7.	γ_2	0.3081	0.1187	2.595	0.01
8.	γ_3	0.6473	0.0724	8.929	0.00
9.	γ_4	1.0288	0.0217	47.28	0.00
10.	γ_5	0.0326	0.1591	0.205	0.84
11.	ρ	0.9960	0.0021	473.8	0.00
12.	σ_1	0.2761	0.0042	65.08	0.00
13.	σ_2	0.6871	0.0569	12.06	0.00
14.	σ_3	0.3567	0.0314	11.33	0.00
15.	σ_4	0.1508	0.0147	10.24	0.00
16.	σ_5	1.1748	0.1648	7.127	0.00

The value for β_1 is not significant and may indicate that the index is not driving the evolution of the daily term spread. Also the value for the GDP lag is not significant suggesting a richer dynamics. Since our goal is not to nowcast the GDP and the fit as presented in Figure 2 is acceptable, we consider that a further modeling of the GDP lag may lead to better results.

We graph below the smoothed coincident index (x_t). The shaded areas depict recessions of Romanian economy, identified as two quarters of negative real growth. According to the data provided by Eurostat, there were three recessions:

1) 2008 Q4 -2009 Q1: GDP growth was -2.47% and -6.16%
2) 2009Q4 – 2010 Q1: GDP growth was -0.32% and -0.69%
3) 2011 Q4 – 2012 Q1: GDP growth was -0.76% and -0.02%.

Since the GDP data are reported with a two month lag, the coincident indicator gives a better estimate of the economic stress with at least two month before the release of the official data. The shaded area for the first recession (2008 Q4 -2009 Q1) is depicted as the period between October 2008 and March 2009. At that time there weren't any GDP forecasts to indicate that a recession is looming.

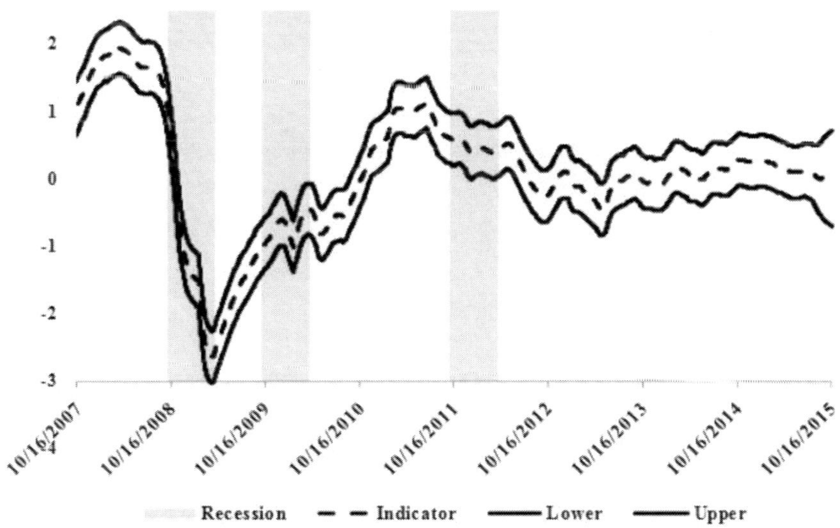

Figure 1. Real-time daily coincident indicator for Romanian business conditions.

The results show that the daily coincident index closely matches the recessions. The index also provides additional information regarding the severity of the recessions and offers highlights on the current state of the business cycle phase which is characterized by a slow but positive index value.

The negative values of the index indicate that the economy is underperforming, while values lower than "-1" show that economy is under a serious economic stress.

The index values start declining on November 2008 and stayed negative until October 2010. The results are consistent with the dynamics of Romanian economy, since it was the hardest hit economy by the economic crisis from Central and Eastern Europe. Since January 2014 the index value turned positive and remained so until Q3 2015 (end of the sample in our calculations). The index suggests a steady but moderate improvement in the business conditions.

Given the fact that the coincident indicator was able to capture in advance the worsening of the economic activity, by providing daily estimates of the underlying business conditions, we consider that the indicator may be a practical tool for policy makers. In this respective it may be used as an early warning instrument.

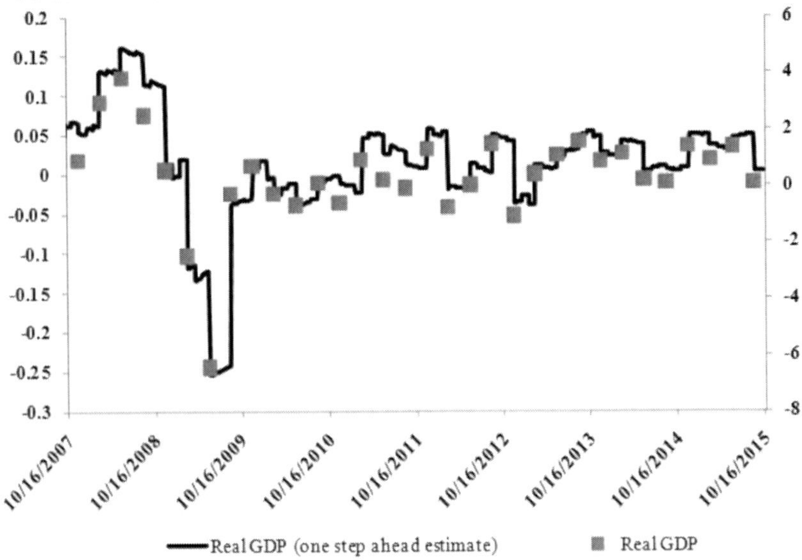

Figure 2. Smoothed (real) GDP estimates versus (real) GDP.

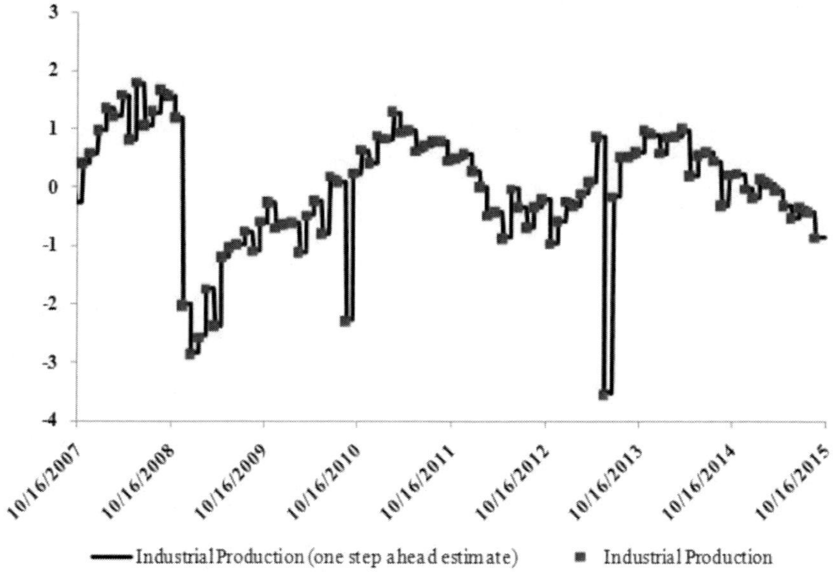

Figure 3. Smoothed Industrial Production estimates versus Industrial Production.

We present below in the Figures 2 and 3 the smoothed estimates of the signal variables along with the signal variables as an additional tool to inspect the fitted results. We present only the signal estimates for industrial production and GDP due to space constraints.

We have identified three stable states for the coincident indicator. The marginal posterior distributions of the parameters estimates with the multimove Gibbs sampler are presented in Table 2.

Table 2. Marginal posterior distributions of the parameters

Parameter	Posterior mean	Posterior std.dev
p_{11}	0.975	0.0049
p_{12}	0.0243	0.0048
p_{21}	0.0214	0.0041
p_{22}	0.9717	0.0047
p_{31}	0.0014	0.0019
p_{32}	0.0262	0.0087

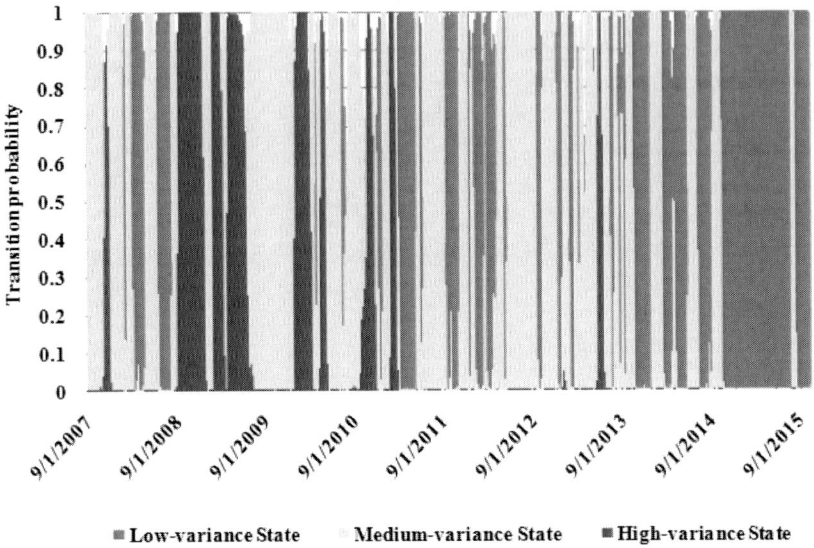

Figure 4. Probability of variance state for the coincident indicator.

In Figure 4 we depict the length of the recessions and the turning points for the business conditions.

As shown in Figure 4, the Romanian economy was already in a medium-variance state in 2008 which can be interpreted as a state of economic overheating due to the high, positive values of the coincident indicator. From October 2008, the indicator started to plummet, entering into negative territory at the beginning of November 2008. The results for Q4 2008 were released in February 2009 and showed a q-o-q decline of GDP of about 2.5%.

CONCLUSION

Some authors have shown that small scale models (Alvarez, Camacho and Perez-Quiros, 2012) yield better results in out-of-sample forecasts than large scale models. Finding the optimal number of macroeconomic/financial time series for estimating in real time the underlying business conditions represents a challenge in the academic research.

In this chapter we have estimated a dynamic factor model with daily, monthly and quarterly data for Romanian economy between Q3 2007 and Q3

2015 in order to extract a daily coincident indicator that is able to "nowcast" (forecast in real-time) the underlying business cycle or business conditions.

Following Aruoba, Diebold and Scotti (2009) we have treated all the observable variables sampled at daily, monthly and quarterly frequencies, as if they were daily observations with missing values, and then we represented the dynamic factor model in a state space framework using Harvey accumulator (1990).

Although we did not use a Markov Switching dynamic for the state variables, the results show that the index was good enough to catch the worsening of the economic activity well before the release of the official statistical data. The model was fitted on the definitive data. As other studies have shown, the revised data can have a substantial effect on the results (Aruoba, 2008).

Also "calling recessions in real time," as Hamilton has shown in his paper (2011), is a very daunting endeavor which cannot be properly done without modeling the variables with a nonlinear process such as a Markov-Switching model.

The daily coincident index matches the recessions, while indicating the severity and length of the recessions. It also provides information on the current state of the business cycle. The current phase of the business cycle (Q3 2015) is characterized by a low but positive index value, suggesting a moderate improvement in the business conditions.

The Romanian economy was the hardest hit CEE economy by the financial crisis of 2007-2009. The coincident index values begin to plummet on November 2008 and remained negative until October 2010, thus registering the longest period of economic stress among Central and Eastern European countries. Since Q1 2014 the index value turned positive and remained so until Q3 2015 which is the end of our sample. A similar result was reported by Caraiani (2010) which estimated the transition probabilities for the Romanian business cycle with a Markov-Switching model for Industrial Production index and found evidence that the economic recession started in Q3 2008 and finished in Q1 2010.

In comparison with a Markov-Switching model which uses data lagged with at least a month (e.g., Industrial Production Index is released with a lag of two months), a real-time coincident index can show in real-time the worsening of the economic activity, thus providing all the benefits associated with an early warning tool.

In the second step we have fitted a Bayesian Markov-Switching model with three states for the coincident indicator. We have identified three stable states for the coincident indicator. In the last eight years the dynamic Romanian economy was mainly characterized by a high and medium variance state. Since Q1 2014 the Romanian economy is characterized by a slow but steady growth in the business conditions, placing the indicator in a low variance state.

The most important result yielded by the dynamic factor model is that the coincident indicator was able to capture in advance the worsening of the economic activity by providing daily estimates of the underlying business conditions.

Acknowledgments

This study was supported by a grant of the Ministry of National Education, CNCS – UEFISCDI, project number PN-II-ID-PCE-2012-4-0631.

References

Albu, Lucian Liviu. A Model to Estimate the Composite Index of Economic Activity in Romania–IEF-RO. *Journal for Economic Forecasting*, 2008, 5.2: 44-50.

Alvarez, Rocio; camacho, Maximo; perez-quiros, Gabriel. Finite sample performance of small versus large scale dynamic factor models. 2012.

Anderson, Richard G.; Gascon, Charles S. Estimating US output growth with vintage data in a state-space framework. *Federal Reserve Bank of St. Louis Review*, 2009, 91.4: 349-69.

Aruoba, S. Borağan; DIEBOLD, Francis X.; SCOTTI, Chiara, Real-Time Measurement of Business Conditions." *Journal of Business and Economic Statistics,2009* 2: 417-27.

Aruoba, S. Borağan. Data revisions are not well behaved. *Journal of money, credit and banking*, 2008, 40.2-3: 319-340.

Banbura, M., and G. Runstler. *A look into the model factor black box. Publication lags and the role of hard and soft data in forecasting GDP.* No. 751. ECB working paper, 2007.

Bańbura, Marta; Modugno, Michele. Maximum likelihood estimation of factor models on datasets with arbitrary pattern of missing data. *Journal of Applied Econometrics*, 2014, 29.1: 133-160.

Boivin, Jean; NG, Serena. Are more data always better for factor analysis?. *Journal of Econometrics*, 2006, 132.1: 169-194.

Brave, Scott A.; Butters, R. Andrew. Gathering insights on the forest from the trees: A new metric for financial conditions. 2010.

Burns, Arthur F.; Mitchell, Wesley C. Measuring business cycles. *NBER Books*, 1946.

Camacho, Maximo; Perez-Quiros, Gabriel. Introducing the euro-sting: Short-term indicator of euro area growth. *Journal of Applied Econometrics*, 2010, 25.4: 663-694.

Caraiani, Petre, et al. Modeling business cycles in the Romanian economy using the Markov switching approach. *Romanian Journal of Economic Forecasting*, 2010, 1: 130-136.

Durbin, James; Koopman, Siem Jan. *Time series analysis by state space methods*. Oxford University Press, 2012.

Evans, Martin DD. *Where are we now? real-time estimates of the macro economy*. National Bureau of Economic Research, 2005.

Giannone, Domenico; Reichlin, Lucrezia; Small, David. Nowcasting: The real-time informational content of macroeconomic data. *Journal of Monetary Economics*, 2008, 55.4: 665-676.

Hamilton, James D. A new approach to the economic analysis of nonstationary time series and the business cycle. *Econometrica: Journal of the Econometric Society*, 1989, 357-384.

Hamilton, James D. Calling recessions in real time. *International Journal of Forecasting*, 2011, 27.4: 1006-1026.

Harvey, Andrew C. *Forecasting, structural time series models and the Kalman filter*. Cambridge University Press, 1990.

Kim, Chang-Jin; Nelson, Charles R. Business cycle turning points, a new coincident index, and tests of duration dependence based on a dynamic factor model with regime switching. *Review of Economics and Statistics*, 1998, 80.2: 188-201.

Nelson, Charles R.; Startz, Richard. Testing for mean reversion in heteroskedastic data based on Gibbs-sampling-augmented randomization. *Journal of Empirical finance*, 1998, 5.2: 131-154.

Mariano, Roberto S.; Murasawa, Yasutomo. A new coincident index of business cycles based on monthly and quarterly series. *Journal of Applied Econometrics*, 2003, 18.4: 427-443.

Stock, James H.; Watson, Mark W. Forecasting using principal components from a large number of predictors. *Journal of the American statistical association*, 2002a, 97.460: 1167-1179.

Stock, James H.; Watson, Mark W. Macroeconomic forecasting using diffusion indexes. *Journal of Business & Economic Statistics*, 2002b, 20.2: 147-162.

Stock, James H.; WATSON, Mark W. *A probability model of the coincident economic indicators*. National Bureau of Economic Research, 1988.

In: Non-Linear Modeling … ISBN: 978-1-63484-932-6
Editors: L. Liviu Albu and P. Caraiani

Chapter 6

THE DYNAMIC RELATIONSHIP BETWEEN THE EQUITY PREMIUM AND UNCERTAINTY

Petre Caraiani*
Institute for Economic Forecasting,
Romanian Academy, Bucharest, Romania

ABSTRACT

Using a wavelet-based decomposition in time and frequency, this paper analyzes the relationship between a key financial variable, the equity premium, and uncertainty. Various measures of equity premium and uncertainty are employed. In general, a positive correlation has been found between the equity premium and uncertainty, becoming negative starting with the financial crisis in 2007-2008. The analysis suggests a weaker relationship during the 1990s at business cycle frequencies, corresponding to a subsample of the Great Moderation, while financial turbulences are depicted through stronger relationships at high frequencies. The relationship becomes strong at almost all frequencies with the onset of the crisis.

Keywords: Equity premium, uncertainty, wavelets, wavelet coherence

* Corresponding Author address: Casa Academiei, Calea 13 Septembrie no. 13, Bucharest, Romania. Email: caraiani@ipe.ro.

INTRODUCTION

A key variable in finance as well as in macro-finance is the equity premium, i.e., the difference between equity return and risk-free return. In finance, the equity premium is the key determinant in portfolio allocation, in estimating capital cost and for many other decisions. A huge literature exists on the dimensions of the equity premium; see Fama and French (2002) or the meta-study by Van Ewijk et al. (2012) for key references. However, most of the literature has focused on deriving the mean equity premium over large historical periods. Beginning in the 1990s, a new line of literature emerged which focused on the presumed decline in the equity premium. Reference papers on this topic are Siegel (1999), Cochrane (1994) and Fama and French (1989). More recently, Lettau et al. (2008) analyzed the decline in the equity premium from the perspective of macroeconomic factors.

In macro-finance, this variable has received a great deal of attention, starting with the reference work by Mehra and Prescott (1984) which derived an equity premium using a real business cycle model. Their work led to an entire body of literature devoted to understanding the so-called equity premium puzzle, which is the difference between the equity premium predicted by the model and the equity premium in the data. Unfortunately, most of this literature has focused more on replicating the mean equity premium rather than on the dynamics in time of the equity premium. See Mehra (2012) for a recent review of this line of research.

This paper studies the dynamics of the equity premium in its relationship with uncertainty. The concept of uncertainty has a long history in economics, dating back to Frank Knight's treatise of 1921. In Knight's original conception, uncertainty is understood as the inability of individuals to forecast the future. Recently, the idea has been revived both conceptually and theoretically through the contribution by Bloom (2009).

A variety of reasons make the current analysis worthwhile. On the one hand, risk is a ubiquitous concept in finance. The very notions of portfolio allocation and decision making contain in themselves the ideas of risk. At the same time, as the difference between two returns, respectively risky and risk-free, the equity premium naturally contains the idea of risk. However, it is less obvious how the equity premium is related to uncertainty. Thus, it is important to know whether fluctuations in the equity premium might theoretically reflect either change in the uncertainty. At the same time, given the multiple facets of the concept of uncertainty, which this paper will explore when discussing the issue of measuring it, it is also important to understand what type of uncertainty influences the equity premium. One might expect that a rising volatility in the equity market, a natural measure of uncertainty, might directly influence the equity premium; however, it is less obvious how a policy measure of uncertainty might influence the equity premium.

The main research question addressed by this paper is whether there exists any kind of relationship between uncertainty and the equity premium. We further offer answers to the questions raised by the existence of such a relationship, namely whether it is frequency dependent and/or time-varying. In doing so, this paper focuses not on the mean value of the equity premium, but rather on this variable's dynamics, in both time and frequency.

But is a time-frequency perspective on the variation and determinants of equity premium justified? This paper argues that it is so, for several reasons. First of all, in a financial market, assets at various levels of maturity are traded simultaneously. Secondly, the equity premium itself contains information on short-run and long-run returns, especially when the risk-free return is determined on the basis of long-run securities.

This paper offers multiple contributions to the literature. First of all, it provides a novel perspective on equity premium dynamics using a wavelet-based decomposition. In contrast to standard filters, the wavelet approach also allows for frequency decomposition. Moreover, while standard Fourier decompositions work only in the frequency space, the wavelet method allows for decomposition in both time and frequency. Such an approach allows us to disentangle high frequency movements, business cycles movements, and long run/low scale movements. A second contribution of the paper is that it relates the changes in equity premium to movements in uncertainty. The equity premium has been studied from various angles, yet its relationship with uncertainty remains poorly known or understood. Finally, a third contribution is that this paper uses several recently proposed measures of uncertainty in a quantitative manner. In doing this, it provides a novel perspective on issues which have remained without a definite answer up until now, namely, as Bloom (2013) underscored, whether and why uncertainty varies and if fluctuations in uncertainty matter in any way.

METHODS

Wavelets were first introduced in economics with the contributions by Ramsey and Lampart (1998a) as well as Ramsey and Lampart (1998b). Although they had been known for quite some time in economics, it is only in the last years that there has been a surge in applying this technique to economics.

In the following paragraphs, I detail the main ingredients of this approach. Two distinct branches exist in wavelet analysis, the discrete approach and the continuous time approach. This paper uses the continuous approach, based on the continuous wavelet transform. My intention is not a detailed presentation of wavelets, which is well beyond the scope of a simple research paper, nor a rigorous presentation, but rather a sketch of the main ideas that will help in understanding the empirical results. I follow the developments of the continuous wavelet transform as discussed in Aguiar-Conraria and Soares (2013, 2014) or Rua (2012).

We start from a given wavelet, denoted by ψ. As shown in the literature, one can write the continuous wavelet transform as follows:

$$W_{s,\tau} = \int_{-\infty}^{\infty} x(t) \frac{1}{\sqrt{s}} \psi^* \left(\frac{t-\tau}{s} \right) dt \tag{1}$$

Here, the symbol * indicates a complex conjugation. This formula is both scale and location dependent, with the scaling parameter s indicating the length of the wavelet, and the location parameter τ indicating the center of the wavelet.

The continuous wavelet transform can basically be applied in two different ways to one or two time series. First, we can apply the so-called wavelet power spectrum to a time series, which can be used to understand that series' variation in time and frequency. One can also apply the cross wavelet transform and, in the end, the wavelet coherence, the last measure indicating the changes in time in the relationship between two series.

Let us start from a time series denoted by x_n, having N observation, with n=0, …,N-1, and a uniform time step δt.

One can compute the wavelet power for the series above by discretizing the integral from (1):

$$W_m^s(s) = \frac{\delta t}{\sqrt{s}} \sum_{n=0}^{N-1} x_n \psi^* \left((n-m) \frac{\delta t}{s} \right) \tag{2}$$

We can move now to the bivariate case, considering a second time series, y_n, with the same number of observations as well as time step. Using a similar approach, we can calculate the cross wavelet transform as:

$$W_n^{xy} = W_n^x W_n^{y*} \tag{3}$$

The so-called cross wavelet power is obtained using the formula $|W_n^{xy}|$. In a univariate case, the wavelet power describes the dynamics of a certain series' variance. In a multivariate case, the cross wavelet power uncovers the dynamics in time and frequency of the covariance between two time series.

The last measure of interest, and the main tool to be used throughout the paper, is the so-called wavelet coherence. This is derived by dividing the cross spectrum to the product of the spectrum of each time series, as seen below:

$$R_n(s) = \frac{\left|S\left(s^{-1}W_n^{xy}(s)\right)\right|}{S\left(s^{-1}\left|W_n^x\right|\right)^{\frac{1}{2}} S\left(s^{-1}\left|W_n^y\right|\right)^{\frac{1}{2}}} \tag{4}$$

Here S stands for a smoothing operator in time and scale.

The continuous wavelet transform also allows an analysis in terms of leading and lagging relationships. The corresponding concept is that of phase difference. This is given by the following equation:

$$\phi_{x,y} = \tan^{-1}\left(\frac{I\{W_n^{xy}\}}{R\{W_n^{xy}\}}\right) \tag{5}$$

where $\phi_{x,y} \in [-\pi, \pi]$.

Following Aguiar-Conraria and Soares (2013, 2014), the phase difference can be interpreted as follows: one can say that the two series co-move when there is a phase difference equal to zero. For a phase difference higher than π, the two series are in an anti-phase relations. Furthermore, in terms of leading and lagging, we say that for $\phi_{x,y} \in \left[-\frac{\pi}{2}, 0\right]$ or $\phi_{x,y} \in \left[\frac{\pi}{2}, \pi\right]$, the series y leads the series x. For $\phi_{x,y} \in \left[-\pi, -\frac{\pi}{2}\right]$ or $\phi_{x,y} \in \left[0, \frac{\pi}{2}\right]$, the time series x leads the time series y.

DATA SELECTION

The data used in this paper refer to rather difficultly measured concepts. A large literature exists on the equity premium, indicating the difficulty of measuring this variable. At the same time, while the literature on uncertainty is at a more incipient level, it still shows that, on the one hand, there is no widely-accepted measure of uncertainty, and on the other, that measured uncertainty essentially depends on the methodology used. See Bloom (2013) for a discussion on how to measure uncertainty.

In order to take into account the relative lack of agreement on how best to measure these two variables, this paper considered various measurements for both equity premium and uncertainty.

For the equity premium, one has to measure both risky return and risk-free returns. In the case of the return on risky assets, the paper uses the CSRP data series on S&P 500, as found in the source for this data series, Welch and Goyal (2008). This measure includes both the real return and the real dividends. Its main advantage is that of being a well-constructed series which has been widely used in both academia and industry.

In the case of risk-free returns, the paper considers both 3-month Treasury bills and 10-year Treasury bonds. For these two series, the paper uses data from the freely available FRED database.

Finally, the equity premium is computed as the difference between the risky return and the risk-free return. As mentioned in the introduction, most of the literature deals with averages over long periods. This paper instead derives a dynamic measure of equity premium. In order to alleviate the problem of year-to-year variation, the paper uses averages over longer periods. Two such periods are considered, one of 10 years and the other of 20 years. These lengths were chosen while considering the tradeoff between ensuring a long enough sub-sample and having enough observations for the subsequent analysis. In this way, we also control for the possible effects of using a certain period for the sub-samples.

Much discussion has been devoted to the question of whether it is preferable to use arithmetic or geometric averages when computing the equity premium. Given this paper's interest in time series dynamics rather than order of magnitude, we focused only on arithmetic averages.

A second issue is selecting the data for uncertainty. The main source for the data is the recent work by Bloom (2013). As shown in the introductory section, uncertainty can be understood as individuals' lack of ability to accurately forecast future events. As such, as Bloom (2013) underscores, a natural empirical measure of uncertainty is the volatility of key variables of interest. In the present paper, I use the volatility of the S&P 500 as a measure for stock market based uncertainty, which is a rather natural measure in the context of studying the equity premium with respect to uncertainty. A second measure of uncertainty is based on news. Proposed by Baker, Bloom and Davis (2013), this measure corresponds to the so-called economic policy uncertainty. In order to measure this, Baker et al. (2013) counted articles in ten leading United States newspapers that met the criteria of containing both the words uncertain/uncertainty and economy/economics.

It must be underscored that these two measures of uncertainty are not only measured using completely different approaches, but are also conceptually different. While the stock market volatility-based measure of uncertainty is a market-based uncertainty measure, the second measure, as the authors acknowledge, is instead a policy-based measure. Figure 1, containing the figures for both measures of uncertainty, better underscores this point.

As already stated, I use the datasets employed and provided by Bloom. See Bloom (2012), as well as Baker et al. (201x) on constructing news-based policy uncertainty. The first dataset, on S&P500 volatility (hereafter VIX), represents a sample between the first quarter of 1991 and the fourth quarter of 2012. The second dataset, on economy policy uncertainty, has a similar sample between the first quarter of 1991 and the fourth quarter of 2012. For the VIX series, data was constructed at quarterly frequency by averaging over the days in a month. The two series are shown in Figure 1. Although data on equity premiums can be built for longer samples, the analysis of co-movement obviously requires equal samples.

RESULTS

The results of the analysis using wavelets coherence are shown in Figures 2 to 9. In Figures 2 to 5, I show the results for the uncertainty measured using the news approach, while Figures 5 to 9 display the stock market volatility-based uncertainty results.

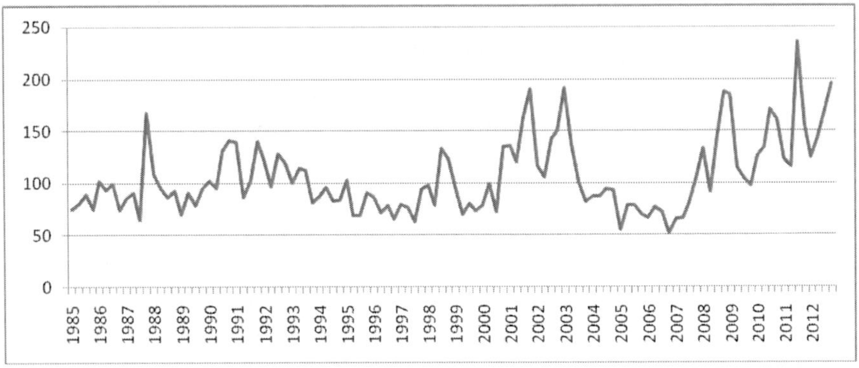

Figure 1a. News based uncertainty.

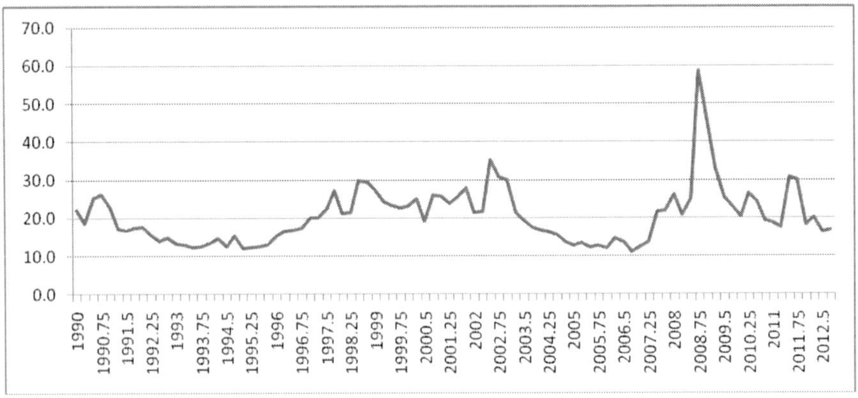

Figure 1b. S&P 500 volatility based uncertainty.

As previously stated, I consider two types of measures for equity premium as well as two samples for moving averages, one of 10 years and one of 20 years.

I turn first to the correlation issue. As stated in the introduction, a phase difference between $-\pi/2$ and $\pi/2$ indicates an in-phase relationship or a positive correlation. It appears that, at both high frequencies and business cycle frequencies, the correlation is mostly positive. Most of the departures from this pattern occur around the end of the Great Moderation (i.e., around 2005).

A second common pattern is again related to the Great Moderation, or at least a sub-sample thereof. Generally speaking, the relationship between uncertainty and the equity premium is weaker during the 1990s (part of the Great Moderation period), especially at business cycle frequencies. Admittedly, the sample in this paper does not include the late 1980s.

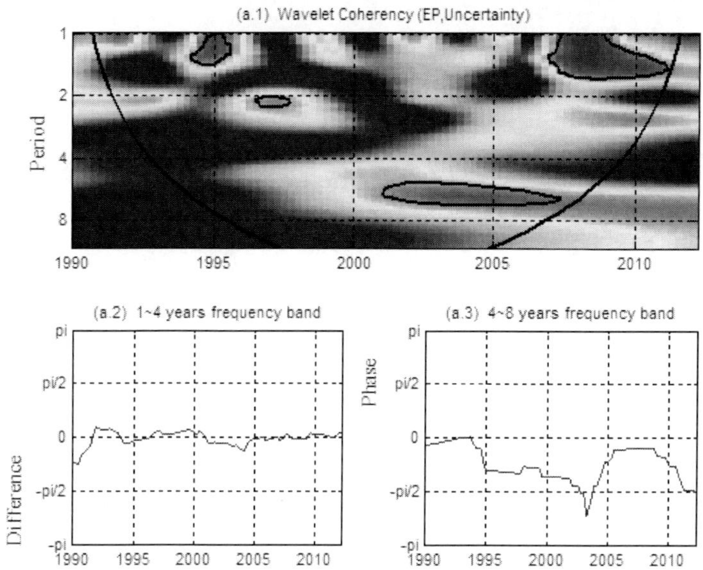

Figure 2. Equity Premium based on Treasury Bills and 10 years average and News Based Uncertainty.

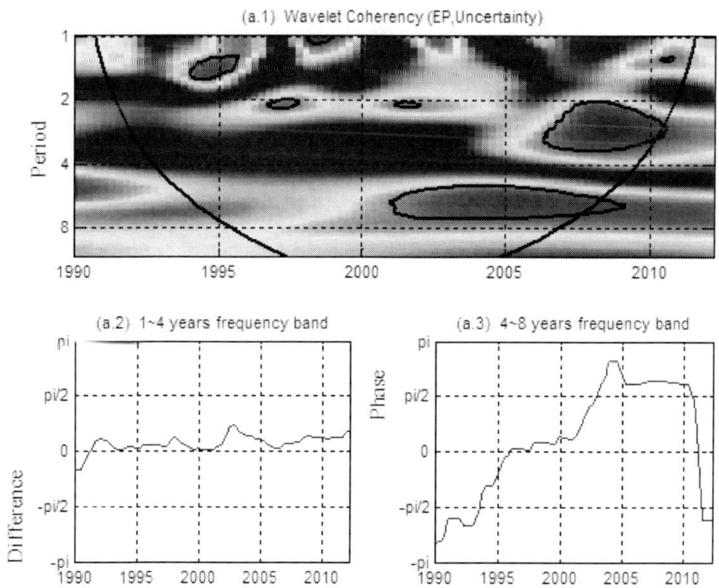

Figure 3. Equity Premium based on Treasury Bills and 20 years average and News Based Uncertainty.

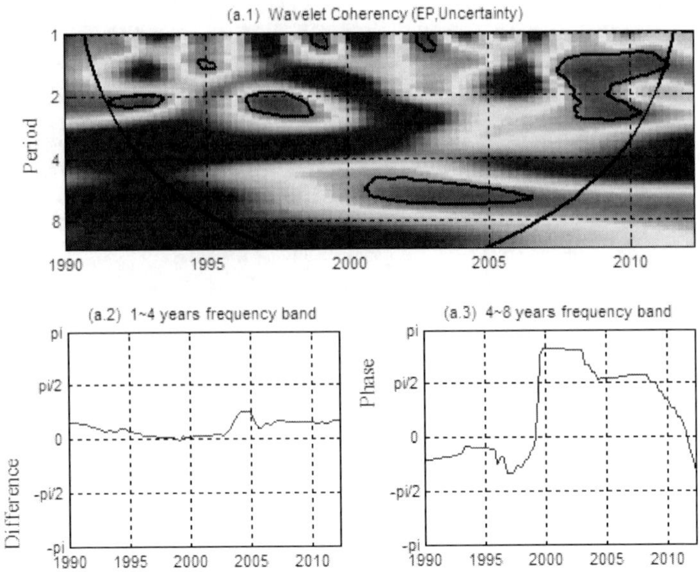

Figure 4. Equity Premium based on Treasury Bonds and 10 years average and News Based Uncertainty.

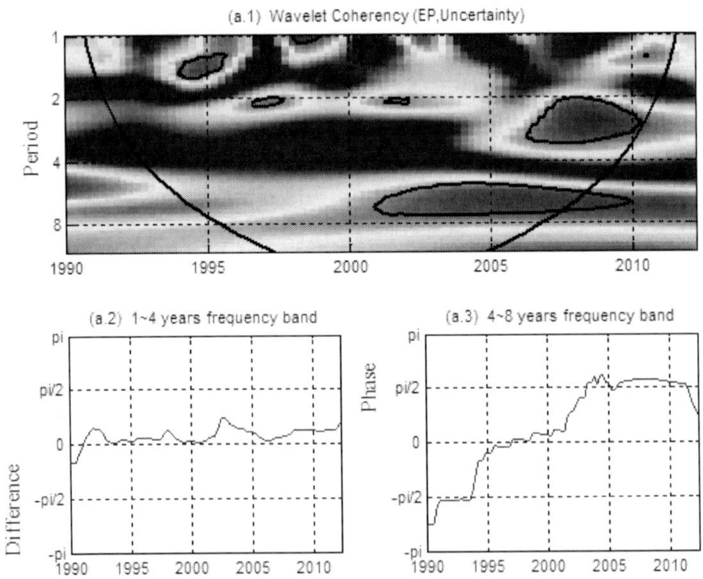

Figure 5. Equity Premium based on Treasury Bonds and 20 years average and News Based Uncertainty.

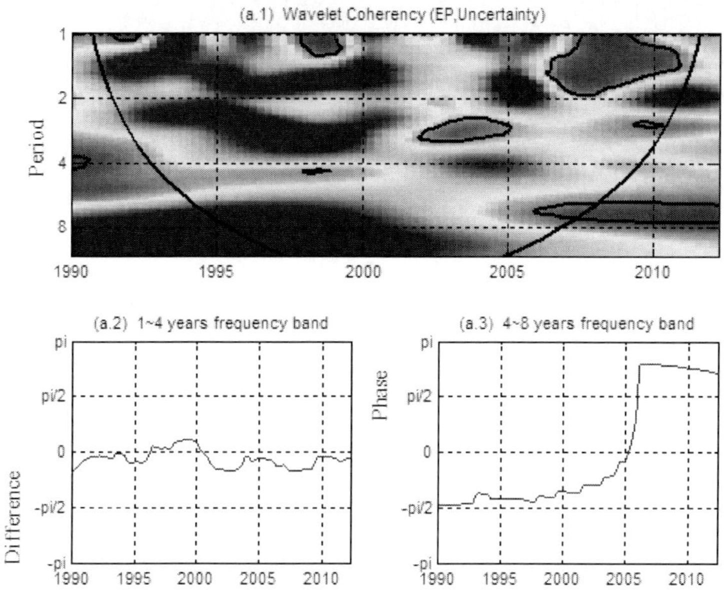

Figure 6. Equity Premium based on Treasury Bills and 10 years average and Stock Market Volatility Based Uncertainty.

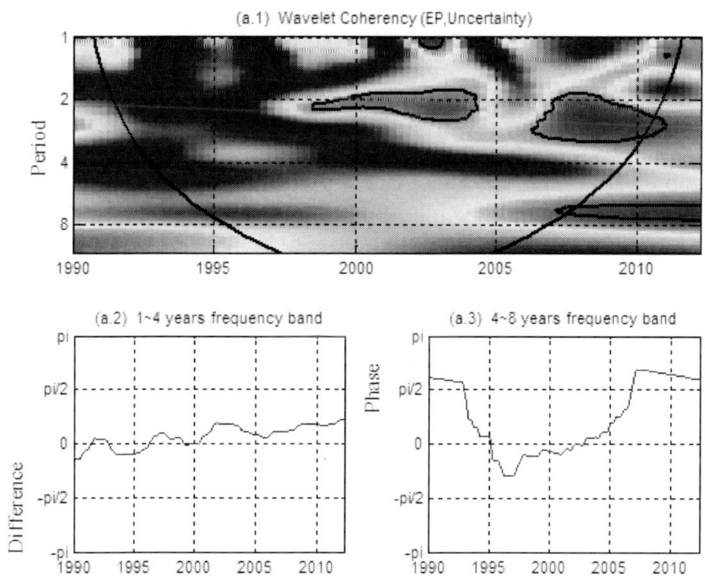

Figure 7. Equity Premium based on Treasury Bills and 20 years average and Stock Market Volatility Based Uncertainty.

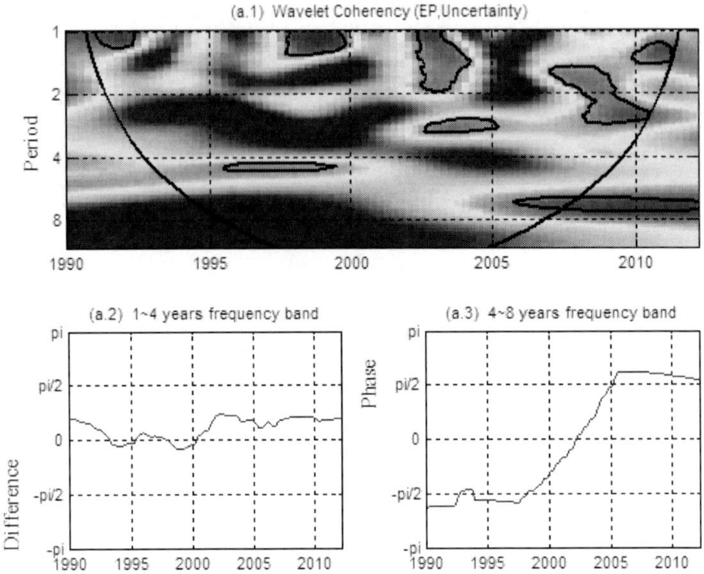

Figure 8. Equity Premium based on Treasury Bonds and 10 years average and Stock Market Volatility Based Uncertainty.

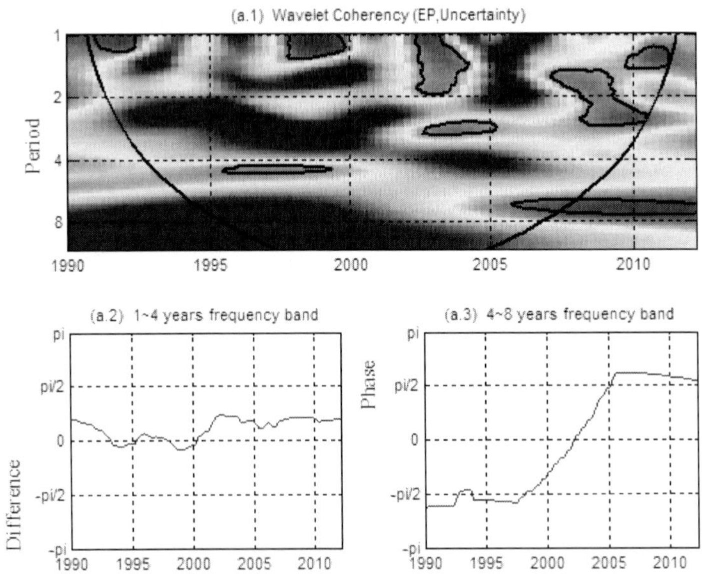

Figure 9. Equity Premium based on Treasury Bonds and 20 years average and Stock Market Volatility Based Uncertainty.

Of course, there are some departures from this generalization, either due to strong relationships at high frequencies, or, in some case, stronger relationships at lower frequencies. An exception to this rule may be given by the last two graphs, which show the relationship between the equity premium based on Treasury Bonds and stock market volatility measure of uncertainty. However, even in this case, overall the relationship is weaker (in the sense of taking into consideration all frequencies) during the sample period corresponding to the Great Moderation than compared to the period of the financial crisis.

A third common pattern found in the various results is that episodes of financial turbulence are usually characterized by movements at high frequencies. This is most obvious in the case of the 1998 episode, but it can also been seen for the 2001 and 2007-2008 episodes. In the latter cases, in general the figures also indicate changes at lower frequencies, usually corresponding to the business cycle frequencies.

Discussion of Results

The main research question of this paper was whether there exists any relationship between uncertainty and equity premium. In light of the results in Section 3, the answer is a clear yes. I also found that this relationship varied in time and in frequency, being weaker during the 1990s and becoming stronger in the 2000s. In general, there is a positive correlation between equity premium and uncertainty, though in some cases, especially starting with the financial crisis, this altered to a negative relationship.

But are these findings in line with what we should expect from a theoretical point of view? First of all, when we recollect the definition of uncertainty, we can understand it as “the inability of individuals to forecast future events.” In a serious financial crisis, such as the one in 2007-2008, uncertainty rose sharply, while the equity premium fell due to the sharp fall in the return of equities; this concurrent contrary movement left the relationship a negative one. But what kind of relationship should we expect in less turbulent times? A rise in uncertainty might lead to more prudent strategies in the market and a flight to bonds, which would translate into lower returns of risk-free assets and a higher equity premium. This is a potential reasonable explanation for the positive correlation between uncertainty and the equity premium for most of the sample.

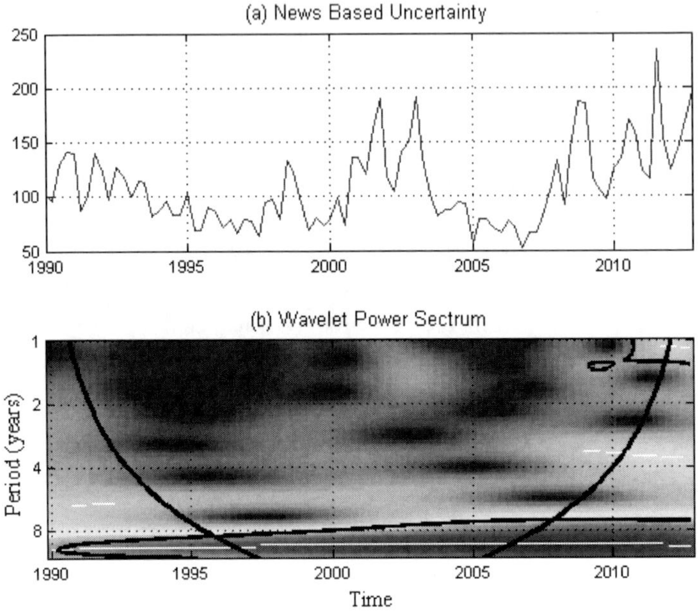

Figure 10. Wavelet Power Spectrum for News Based Uncertainty.

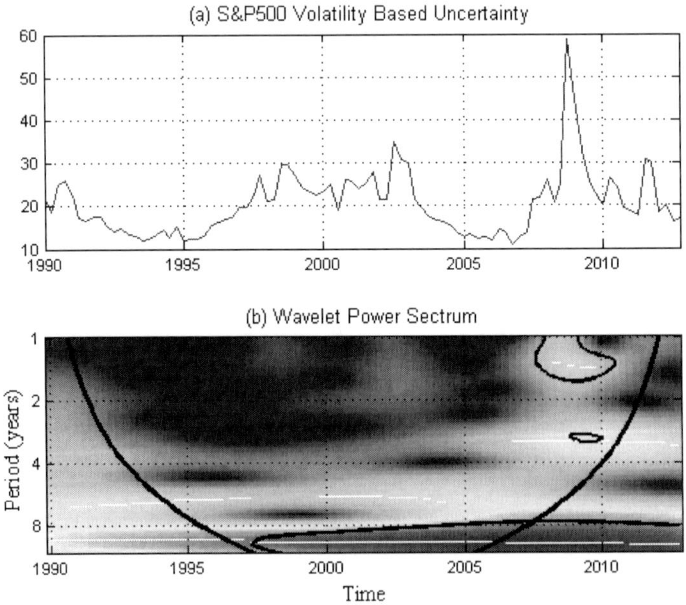

Figure 11. Wavelet Power Spectrum for Stock Market Volatility Based Uncertainty.

But why did the sign of the relationship change at the onset of the financial crisis? A potential explanation is that although there was a flight to safe havens, there was even a sharper fall in stock market returns, resulting in a lower equity premium and thus a negative relationship.

A secondary interest of this paper was the quantitative use of various uncertainty measures and a contribution to the understanding if and why uncertainty varies. Figures 10 and 11 show the wavelet power spectrum for the two measures of uncertainty used throughout this paper. Surprisingly, for both measures, most of the variation up to the mid-2000s, which roughly corresponds to the end of the Great Moderation, is due to low frequency movements. Starting with early 2000, there is an increasing role for movements at business cycle frequencies. Again, the crisis in 2007-2008 and is depicted through higher frequency movements.

These results show that uncertainty does vary in time. They also show that the movements at different frequencies are quite significant and that they changed their relative importance in time. Furthermore, the changes in uncertainty can be organically linked to various economic episodes. It is obvious that financial crisis episodes, especially dramatic ones like the financial crisis in 2007-2008, lead to an increase in uncertainty. It is also well documented that during the Great Moderation, there was a decrease in the volatility of the key macroeconomic and financial variables. Since volatility is naturally linked to uncertainty, uncertainty had a lower variation during the Great Moderation. This is obvious from the two figures in Figure 1, the only exception being the rise in uncertainty during the dotcom stock market crisis in early 2000 (at least in the case of news-based uncertainty).

Finally, the research also shows that variations in uncertainty can be linked to a key variable in finance, the equity premium. As already highlighted at the beginning of the discussion section, insofar as uncertainty reflects changing information about the economic and financial environment, we should expect changes in uncertainty to be reflected in the decision of agents either in the macro-economy or in the financial markets.

CONCLUSION

This paper provided a new perspective on the variation in equity premium by considering an analysis in time and frequency. Furthermore, the equity premium was analyzed in its relationship with uncertainty. Different measures of equity premium were considered, by varying the length of the mobile sample (using averages over 10 or 20 years respectively), the measures of risk-free returns (3-month Treasury bills or 10-year Treasury bonds) as well as the uncertainty measures (news-based or based on stock market volatility).

Surprisingly, in spite of the variety of specifications, a few patterns emerged. The various episodes of increased stock market turbulence (1998, 2001, 2007-2008) reveal strong correlations between equity premium and uncertainty at high frequencies. For the latter episodes, especially the 2007-2008 financial crisis, turbulence also appears at business cycle frequencies. Furthermore, although the results vary according to the measure of uncertainty used and the sub-samples used to determine the equity premium, a weaker relationship is depicted in the first part of the sample, which corresponds to a sub-sample of what is known as the Great Moderation.

Another significant result is that this paper was able to link variations in the uncertainty to variations in the equity premium. Although it is quite natural to assume that variations in risk should translate into variations in equity premium, the relationship with uncertainty is both less studied and less obvious. Through a mutual analysis in time and frequency, it was possible to uncover the changing relationship between uncertainty and the equity premium and link it to various episodes, like the Great Moderation, or the financial crisis of 2007-2008.

Future research should attempt to quantify the different roles of risk and uncertainty in shaping the dynamics of the equity premium. Structural approaches to model the relationship between uncertainty and the equity premium should also be pursued.

ACKNOWLEDGMENTS

This study was supported by a grant of the Ministry of National Education, CNCS – UEFISCDI, project number PN-II-ID-PCE-2012-4-0631.

REFERENCES

Aguiar-Conraria, Luis and Maria J. Soares. 2014. “The Continuous Wavelet Transform: beyond uni- and bivariate analysis.” *Journal of Economic Surveys* 28(2): 344-375.

Aguiar-Conraria, Luis, Martins, Manuel and Maria J. Soares. 2013. "The yield curve and the macro-economy across time and frequencies." *Journal of Economic Dynamics & Control* 36: 1950-1970.

Baker, Scott, Nicholas Bloom, and Steven Davis. 2012. "Measuring economic policy uncertainty." Stanford University mimeo.

Bloom, Nicholas. 2009. "The impact of uncertainty shocks." *Econometrica* 77 (3): 623-685.

Bloom, Nicholas. 2013. "Fluctuations in Uncertainty." Stanford University mimeo.

Cochrane, JohnH. 1994. "Permanent and transitory components of GNP and stock prices." *Quarterly Journal of Economics* 109: 241–265.

Fama, Eugene F. and Kenneth R. French. 2002. "The Equity Premium." *Journal of Finance* 57(2): 637-659.

Fama, Eugene F., and Kenneth R. French. 1989. "Business conditions and expected returns on stocks and bond." *Journal of Financial Economics* 25: 23–49.

Knight, Frank. 1921. *Risk, Uncertainty and Profit.* Boston, MA: Hart, Schaffner & Marx.

Lettau, Martin, Sydney C. Ludvigson, and Jessica A. Wachter. 2008. "The Declining Equity Premium: What Role Does Macroeconomic Risk Play?" *Review of Financial Studies* 21(4): 1653-1687.

Mehra, Rajnish, and Edward Prescott. 1985. "The equity premium: A puzzle." *Journal of Monetary Economics* 15: 145–161.

Mehra, Rajnish. 2012. "Consumption Based Asset Pricing Models." *Annual Review of Finance and Economics* 4: 385-409.

Ramey, Gary and Valerie Ramey. 1995. "Cross-country evidence on the link between volatility and growth." *American Economic Review* 85(5): 1138–1151.

Ramsey, James and Camille Lampart. 1998a. "The Decomposition of Economic Relationships by the Scale Using Wavelets: Money and Income." *Macroeconomic Dynamics* 2: 49-71.

Ramsey, James and Camille Lampart. 1998b. "The Decomposition of Economic Relationships by Time Scale Using Wavelets: Expenditure and Income." *Studies in Nonlinear Dynamics and Econometrics* 3 (4): 23-42.

Rua, Antonio. 2012. "Money Growth and Inflation in the Euro Area: A Time-Frequency View." *Oxford Bulletin of Economics and Statistics* 74(6): 875-885.

Siegel, Jeremy J. 1999. "The shrinking equity premium." *Journal of Portfolio Management* 26: 10–17.

Van Ewijk, Casper, Henry L.F. de Groot and Coos Santing. 2012. "A meta-analysis of the equity premium." *Journal of Empirical Finance* 19(5): 819-830.

Welch, Iwo and Amit Goyal. 2008. "A Comprehensive Look at The Empirical Performance of Equity Premium Prediction." *Review of Financial Studies* 21(4): 1455-1508.

EDITOR CONTACT INFORMATION

Dr. Lucian Liviu Albu
Academician
Institute for Economic Forecasting
Romanian Academy, Romania
Tel: +40-740017959
Email: albul@ipe.ro

Dr. Petre Caraiani
Institute for Economic Forecasting
Romanian Academy, Romania
Email: petre.caraiani@gmail.com
caraiani@ipe.ro

INDEX

D

E

F

G

H

I

J

K

L

M

N

O

P

Q

R

S

T

U

V

W

Y

Following the last economic and financial crisis, there is strong motivation for academics to better explain the connection between the stock market and the macroeconomy. This book aims at fulfilling this need with an accent on the case of emerging markets in Central and Eastern Europe. The book generally focuses on nonlinear techniques.

The book consists of several chapters, each using state-of-the-art techniques in modeling that address specific issues related to the focus of the book. The topics range from studying the transmission mechanism of monetary policy in CEE economies, to issues like the impact of quantitative easing on the emerging markets or network based approaches that advance our understanding of the financial relationships in these markets. The book also includes a paper on the wavelets modeling of the relationship between uncertainty and equity premium. Given the nature of the CEE economies, i.e. aspiring Euro Area members, a special chapter is dedicated to convergence issues and the nonlinear relationship between economic growth and finance.

Overall, in the present context of the post-financial crisis, this book constitutes a step forward in the modeling of the linear and nonlinear relationships between the financial markets and the macroeconomy, especially in an unstable context and for the particular case of emerging economies.

nov
publish
www.novapublisher

9781634849326
TP
APEX